A HISTORY OF THE AMBROSIANA

A History of the Ambrosiana

ANGELO PAREDI

Translated by

Constance and Ralph McInerny

Published for
THE MEDIEVAL INSTITUTE
UNIVERSITY OF NOTRE DAME
by the
UNIVERSITY OF NOTRE DAME PRESS

To

THEODORE M. HESBURGH, C.S.C.

In recognition of and with gratitude
for his support of the Medieval Institute
and its various projects over many decades.

CONTENTS

I

ORIGINS

The idea for the Ambrosiana came to Count Federico Borromeo while he was staying in Rome. Insistent friends and relatives had persuaded him to go to the Eternal City in 1586 at the age of twenty-two. It was their intention that he should take up the positions in the Curia and the Church left vacant by the untimely death of his famous cousin, the Cardinal of St. Praxides and Archbishop of Milan. Federico came to Rome in the autumn of 1586 and remained there for nine years. He was created cardinal by Sixtus V in December of 1587. Elected Archbishop of Milan, he returned to his native city in the summer of 1595. However, after only twenty months residence, because of a serious dispute with the Spanish Governor Juan Velasquez over ecclesiastical jurisdition, he returned to Rome in April, 1597 and remained there another four years. Eventually, in June 1603, Federico returned to Milan and that same year suddenly began asking men in various places to trace and acquire codices and books. In 1603 construction of the library building began.

No one in the indolent Spanish Milan of the Sixteenth Century was concerned with libraries. But in the Roman atmosphere in which the young Cardinal Borromeo had lived, codices and old books were objects of intense interest.

The *Relatione* written in Rome in 1598-99 by Alexander d'Este says that Cardinal Borromeo was a "pupil at Vallicella." In fact he was educated at Pavia, but Borromeo was so frequent a visitor in the house of Father Phillip Neri, the famous Oratorian, at Vallicella, that he was commonly thought to be one of the young men who emerged from the community of Father Phillip. But in the years of Federico's Roman sojourn, those at Vallicella were mainly concerned with studying the ancient history of the Church. One of them, Caesar Baronius, worked from morning till evening on the codices of the Vatican Library and, at night, at home, wrote the *Annales*, the monumental work meant to be the Catholic reply to the *centuriatores* of Magdeburg who gathered in thirteen superb volumes (l559-1574) a variety of poisonous and violent attacks on Catholicism and Rome. At the beginning of the second volume of the Annales, which appeared in 1590, there is a letter of dedication to Cardinal Borromeo. Achille Ratti, in a little work of 1910, showed how close and fraternal the friendship between Borromeo and Baronius was.

On the other hand, Federico was in Rome as a cardinal of the Curia in the very years that the biblical codices became an anguishing and thorny problem for the Roman Curia. The Fathers of the Council of Trent in 1546 declared "authentic" the Latin Vulgate translation and asked the Roman Pontiff to publish an accurate edition of it. The undertaking was anything but easy and for a decade popes charged various commissions with the task. Finally Sixtus V with his tremendous energy took the codices into his own hands and set about correcting the text which the last commission had submitted to him. The Sistine Vulgate appeared in May, 1590. The publication aroused a storm of criticism which had not yet calmed when, a few months after the new Bible appeared, Pope Sixtus died. The new Pope, Gregory XIV , in January 1591, assigned the revision of the Sistine Vulgate to a commission and asked Cardinal Borromeo to take part in it. Gregory XIV having died, the newly elected Pope Clement VIII, in the first months of 1592, put into the hands of Cardinals Borromeo and Valier the tangled question of the Sistine Bible; they had the Jesuit Francis Toleto prepare a new edition which appeared in November, 1592. For the completion of this thorny enterprise the counsel of Robert Bellarmine was decisive: what he wrote about the edition of the Sistine-

Clementine Vulgate is preserved in a codex that Cardinal Federico donated to the Ambrosiana.

In short, Borromeo was made aware in Rome of the importance of culture for any efficacious defense of a Christian civilization menaced not only by the barbarism of the Turks but also by the fragmenting theories of innovators. At the end of 1587 a man who had been a good friend of St. Charles, Cardinal Augustin Valier, addressed an exhortation to the twenty-three year old Federico, later published by Mai, with suggestions on how he might best employ his youthful energies. Among other things he said, "... interest in Roman antiquity is laudable, but more laudable still is the study of ancient books. Good books do not waste our time as most people do; books are friends which enrich us as much as we desire. You should, then, Cardinal Borromeo, collect a great quantity of books, build a library worthy of your noble soul, and spend without stint all the money necessary for it." While in Rome, Cardinal Borromeo could watch the construction of the splendid new Vatican Library ordered by Sixtus V, and see the establishment of the Vatican Press, another work of Sixtus V, just as the vaulting of the dome of St. Peter's was accomplished, twenty-four years after the death of Michelangelo, and the Vatican Library acquired the conspicuous additions of the library of Cardinal Carafa (1591) and the still more important and precious one of Fulvio Orsini (1600). These are the antecedents which explain the founding of the Ambrosiana.

The effort of Cardinal Borromeo to collect books and above all manuscripts for the Ambrosiana began even before 1601 and continued intensively throughout his years in Milan. He sent his secretary, Grazio M. Grazi, to the principal cities of Italy; Antonio Olgiato of Lugano traveled through Germany, Belgium, Holland and France; Francesco Bernadino Ferrari traversed Spain. Antonio Salmazia, in order to acquire Greek codices, established himself for a time on Corfu and from there ordered books from Albania, the Peloponnese, the island of Eubaeus, Zante and Macedonia. Giovanni Battista Besozzi and Fabio Leuco scoured Naples. Michele Maronita went to Syria and other parts of the East. To Bobbio, the cardinal sent the noble Gian Giacomo Valeri, *canonico della Scala*. The cardinal provided these men with money and personal promissory notes; all served the noble cause with ardor, intelligence and faithfulness. Salmazia was particularly lucky in being able to acquire at Chio the complete library of Michele Sofiano. Francesco Notara, on the other hand, spent on food money given to buy books. Other people too helped Federico in the effort: bishops, missionaries, businessmen, Genoese ship captains, Tuscans and Neopolitans; in a special way the Venetian residents of Alexandria, Cairo, Cyprus, Damascus and Aleppo. Finally, the cardinal constantly employed agents in Rome.

Of enormous importance was the acquisition of the Bobbio manuscripts. Unfortunately the library of Bobbio had been visited and sacked by various humanists since 1493. Cardinal Federico's envoy succeeded in persuading the monks of the high aim of the new Milanese foundation and in 1605 seventy-six codices were brought from Bobbio to Milan. Several of these codices are overwritten, or palimpsests; that is they consist of folios written, for instance, in the seventh century on parchment already used for writing in the sixth century, then cleaned so they could be used again. The fragments of a Bible written in the Gothic language in sixth century northern Italy when it was governed by the Goths are famous. The coming of the Lombard horde changed everything. When the monks of Bobbio began again in the seventh century to write codices, no one could understand a book in the Gothic language. It was useless. So they cleaned the Gothic Bible and used the parchment to transcribe for themselves a commentary of Jerome on Isaiah. Later we will speak of Mai's discoveries in the Bobbio codices.

Another boon for the Ambrosiana was the acquisition of a good part of the library of Gian Vincenzo Pinelli. This bibliophile had collected a treasury of manuscripts and books at Padua. When he died in 1601, he left his library to a nephew, Duke Cosmo, who lived in Naples. However, before the crates full of books could leave for Naples, the Venetian senate confiscated two hundred volumes of political writings on the pretext that they had been copied from the archives of the Venetian government. Then, as a cautionary measure, the crates were loaded not on one but on three ships to be transported to the Neapolitan heir. One of these was captured by Turkish pirates off Ancona.

The brigands had hoped for rich booty and, finding the crates contained only books, in rage and delusion they pitched the codices into the sea. Fishermen of the Fermo region, finding many parchment folios in their nets, used them as windows in their houses until a decree of the Pontifical Prefect of the area ordered them turned in. It was thus possible to recover twenty-two of the crates, though eleven were lost forever. Of these eleven, eight contained codices, two were filled with prints and drawings and one contained scientific instruments. When the inheritance got to Naples, the heir was dead, and it was then put up for sale. Unfortunately many wanted to acquire them. Cardinal Borromeo sent Grazi to Naples.

In January 1607, he wrote Federico that he had seen the books and they were so damaged from the long voyage that "he would spend nothing without having scrutinized them twice or more." The famous Pinellian library was put on auction in Naples in June, 1608 and was acquired by Cardinal Borromeo for 3050 ducats. Legal difficulties arose. Finally more than five hundred Pinellian codices, together with many other printed volumes, packed in seventy boxes, were transported to Milan on nine wagons in 1609. To grasp the importance of the acquisition it is enough to say that the famous illustrated Homer, precious texts of Plautus, Cicero and Horace, as well as the correspondence of Bembo and Lucrezia Borgia, with the famous lock of hair, are Pinellian.

Federico himself acquired a large group of codices in Milan from the library of the cathedral chapter; another group from the Augustinian convent of Santa Maria Incoronata also in Milan. Other manuscripts were obtained in small number, even singly, from learned private parties or from more or less informed heirs. Erstwhile owners of manuscripts now in the Ambrosiana were Maffeo Vegio, Gerolamo Mercuriale, Francesco Ciceri, Pier Candido Decembrio, Gaudenzio and Filippo Merula, Ottavio Perrari, Senator Cesare Rovida and many others, famous and obscure.

Thus came into being a large mass of nearly fifteen thousand manuscripts of which not a few, Latin, Italian, Greek, Oriental and other languages, are truly precious. At least two hundred of these are illuminated, that is, decorated with figures and stories. Several codices are often bound in one volume: thus the 2205 Greek manuscripts make 1098 volumes.

For printed books, Cardinal Borromeo went to the best publishers in Italy and other European countries and put together a choice body of nearly thirty thousand volumes which formed the first nucleus of the growing library.

NOTES

For the biography of Cardinal Federico Borromeo and its sources, see Paolo Bellezza, *Federico Borromeo*, Milan, 1931 as well as the interesting information given by L. Pulle in F. Calvi's *Famiglie Notabili Milanesi*, Vol. II, Milan, 1881, Table X. ---For the years in Rome, see G. Gabrieli, *"Federico Borromeo in Rome,"* in *Archivio della Societa Romana di Storia Patria*, Tomes LVI-LVII, Rome, 1933-34, pp. 157-217. ---On Federico's controversy with the Spanish authorities in Milan, see M. Bendiscioli in *Storia di Milano*, X, Milan, 1957, pp. 308 ff. ---The *Relatione* of the confidant of Alexander d'Este was published by L. Pastor, *Storia dei Papi* XI, Rome, 1929, pp. 759 ff. ---Achille Ratti's piece on Baronius can be found in the volume *Per Cesare Baronio: Scritti Varinel III Centenario*, Rome, 1911, pp. 179-254. ---On the Clementine Vulgate, see Pastor, *op. cit.* XI, Rome, 1919, p. 481 ff. ---Valier's exhortation was published by A. Mai, *Script. vet. nova coll.*, VI, Rome, 1832, pp. 281-304. ---Several letters from men deputized by Federico to buy codices and books are reported by A. Ceruti, *La Biblioteca Ambrosiana*, Milan, 1880, pp. 11-29. ---See the history of the Pinelli library in A. Rivolta, *Catalogo dei Codici Pinelliani*, Milan, 1933. ---Fabio Leuco describes the sale at auction of the Pinelli library in a letter to Federico; see Ms. G 198 bis inf., fol 255. ---On the sale of codices from the cathedral library, see A. Paredi, *La Bibloteca del Pizolpasso*, Milan, 1961. ---Federico wanted there to be a printing press in the library too: it was in operation from 1617 to 1650 and again from 1747 to 1753 and finally from 1861 to 1863.

II

THE FIRST BUILDING

Cardinal Federico, prior to deciding how and where to house the books and codices he had collected, consulted various architects, but the definitive design seems to have been the work of Francesco Richino or Lelio Buzzi. Construction began in June, 1603. Borromeo had acquired three small houses bordered on the south by the Piazza San Sepolcro, on the west by what is now called Via dell' Ambrosiana, on the north by a school founded by Stefano Taverna, on the east by the small church of Santa Maria della Rosa maintained by the Dominicans, and further south by the house of the Oblate Fathers and their church of San Sepolcro. They were miserable houses. In 1883 Canetta published the history of the *Pio Istituto di Santa Corona*, founded in the same area, and cited a chronicle of the Santa Corona: "such are the places near the church and pigs and cheeky prostitutes inhabit the region."

After the houses were razed, there was a narrow strip of land 13,60 meters in breadth and 70 meters long. Construction had hardly begun when disputes arose. Plans of Richino have been preserved which show a facade somewhat different from that actually built. In the summer of 1604 Borromeo submitted the project to the examination of another architect, Alessandro Tesauro of Torino, who suggested that the length of the rectangular Grand Salon be reduced to permit the inclusion of an atrium. Perhaps because of these disputes, Lelio Buzzi abandoned the commission in September 1604.

A small atrium was in fact constructed, 6,50 meters by 4, illumined by seven windows. The Grand Salon ended up being 26 meters long, 13,60 wide and 15 high, with two large semicircular windows opened in the walls of the heading, above the cornice on which the vault reposes. On the same axis as the Grand Salon a small square courtyard was surrounded on three sides by a portico which, on one side, gave access to stairs leading either to the upper quarters or to a basement designed for keeping archival papers as well as prohibited books; on the other side, the portico gave access to the meeting room of the Trustees. Beyond this, still on the same axis, is the room in which manuscripts are conserved. These areas behind the Grand Salon are half as high as it, so as not to block light entering the semicircular window, as can be seen in the plate on pages 96-7 of Volume Four of Latuada.

In building his library in such a way that all walls are available for the placement of books, Cardinal Borromeo was inspired by the library of the Escorial opened by Phillip II in 1584. The libraries of the fifteenth and sixteenth centuries retained the medieval system of the chained book: thus the rooms had to be full of lecterns to which books were attached and readers had to stay close to them. The Malatestiana of Cesena (1452) was like this, as were the Laurenziana of Florence, that of Monte Oliveto and the Vaticana of Sixtus IV (1475). Girolamo Borsieri, in his supplement to the *Nobilta di Milano*, printed in 1619 by Paolo Morigi, marvels at precisely this that "the Ambrosiana is not half full of tables to which books are tied or chained as is customary in monastery libraries, but is surrounded by high shelves on which the books are arranged proportionally." Thus in the architectural plans for his library, Federico already shows that he means to make books accessible. Borromeo's liberality, so praised by Manzoni, should not be considered a complete innovation; even in the Vatican Library at the end of the fifteenth century, though books were chained, they were readily given to borrowers, though each, alas, with its chain attached. In his library, Federico would follow the absolute rule, already laid down by Sir Thomas Bodley for the library at Oxford, that neither codices nor printed books should be given to any borrower.

Sassi gives us a precise description of how books were to be shelved: "this room is completely full of books, without any chance of disturbance, with the exception of a door through which one enters and another opposite through which one goes to the other rooms ... The arrangement of shelves on which the books are kept involves a division into *superiore* and inferior. In the *inferiore* or lower level are placed folio books in open hazelwood cabinets with fine carvings which do not however detract from the books themselves. Seven of these cabinets are on the north side and seven on the south .... Two others are on the east, two somewhat smaller on the west .... Each contains nine shelves of books in diminishing proportion .... They are covered with wooden latticed screens up to the fifth shelf, taller than any human, lest someone should steal a book, and they are locked, leaving the books nonetheless visible because of the screens. The *superiore* is not protected in this way ... In the corners of the *inferiore*, there are four little closets jutting out ... and in one of them is a spiral staircase for getting to the *superiore* ...."

Above the wooden cornice topping the cabinets runs a series of portraits of eighty-two famous Christians framed in plaster and gold. Ten meters above the floor, a rich molding establishes the placement of the vault in the longitudinal direction. Divided by great squares and richly decorated with stucco and gilt, it reaches at its summit a height of fifteen meters above ground level.

NOTES

On the architects of the first Federican buildings, see Gentile Pagani in *Arch. St. Lomb.*, 1892, pp. 900 ff. and L. Gramatica in the opusculum, *L'Ambrosiana*, Milan, Fratelli Treves, 1923, pp.20 ff. ---On the innovations at the Escorial and the Ambrosiana, see J. W. Clark, *The Care of Books*, Cambridge, 1901, pp. 267 ff. ---G. A. Sassi's description is in S. Latuada, *Descrizione di Milano*, Tome IV, Milan, 1738, pp. 93-120.

III

THE LIBRARIANS

Anticipating the completion of the building, having brought together a considerable number of manuscripts and books, Borromeo officially founded the library with a notary's instrument dated September 7, 1607. In a conspicuous example of modesty, he did not wish his foundation to be named after either himself or his family but to be called the Ambrosian Library after Milan's most beloved saint.

Even before the official inauguration, Cardinal Federico gave thought to the men who would be custodians of the cultural and scientific treasures collected in the Ambrosiana and make them fruitful. He decided on two colleges, that of the *Conservatori* or Trustees and that of the *Dottori* or Scholars, colleges governed by appropriate constitutions researched and put into final form by himself. These would insure the functioning of his institution for three and a half centuries despite political disturbances and oppressive foreign occupation. Unfortunately, the student college, which was to provide recruits for the future, did not survive, though it indicates how great the cardinal's ambitions were. No more did the college for the study of the three languages, Greek, Latin and Italian, survive. For that matter, the scholarships he requested and obtained from the Holy See for youths of proved ability, who were to study first in the diocesan seminary and then come to serve the library, did not last.

The proper task of the *Conservatori* in Federico's mind was and is wisely to administer and increase the means he left for sustaining his foundation. The eldest member of the Borromeo family was a *conservatore* for life; five year terms were to be served by men elected from the cathedral chapter and from the pastors of the city. He provided for the future of the institution variously, both with buildings and with land. Unfortunately, for a number of reasons, and perhaps especially because of the heavy expenses brought on by the plague of 1630, these bequests were deplenished, as Cardinal Federico himself noted in an addendum to the Constitution written toward the end of his life. Hence he entrusted the fortune and life of his Ambrosiana to "the magnanimity and liberality" of the city of Milan.

Alessandro Manzoni wrote, "Federico brought together in the library a College of Scholars (there were nine, given pensions by him for life, but afterward, the funds not permitting this, they were restricted to two); their task was to cultivate various studies, theology, history, literature, ecclesiastical antiquity, oriental languages, with the added obligation that each publish some work on the matter assigned him." To find the first Scholars, and in so large a number, was no easy matter. "It suffices to say," Manzoni continues, "that, of the nine Scholars, eight were taken from the alumni of the seminary. From this one can gather Cardinal Federico's judgment of reputations made in research at that time, a judgment shared by posterity, as the oblivion into which they have fallen indicates." The Scholars were to take care of the books and manuscripts, make them available to the learned community, exchange reports with the erudite, especially foreigners, to extract fruit from the bibliographical riches entrusted to them, each in a limited and special field, according to the motto *singuli singula*, that is, "Let each devote himself to his allotted task." It was their duty to give public proof of their private studies in printed works. This conception of the library remains fully valid today.

Cardinal Federico wanted a solemn and festive celebration to mark the opening of the Ambrosiana. Some noticed that by bestowing such wealth on his library, Borromeo meant to fill a growing need of the city. The fact was that Rome and Florence, Venice, Urbino and Cesena could boast of already famous libraries while at Milan there was none or as bad as none. The great libraries that the Visconti and Sforzas had collected in their castle in Pavia had been, alas, taken to France at the fall of Ludovico il Moro in 1499. Perhaps with things like these in mind, on the afternoon of December 7, 1609, the feast of St. Ambrose,

Cardinal Federico invited the whole city as if to a holiday. The senate took part in full panoply, as did the magistrature, the college of doctors, civil and clerical leaders and such a crowd of people that neither the church of San Sepolcro, where the ceremony took place, nor the piazza and streets flanking the church, could hold them.

NOTES

There were several 17th Century editions of the *Constitutiones Collegii et Bibliothecae Ambrosianae*; Francesco Bentivoglio published an Italian version in 1835 which was reprinted in 1933. ---Manzoni's famous remarks about Cardinal Federico and the Ambrosiana are in Chapter XXII of *I Promessi Sposi*. ---The most important publications by Scholars of the Ambrosiana in the 17th Century are those of Ripamonti and those of Antonio Giggei (Giggeius) who in 1632 published a *Thesaurus Linguae Arabicae* in four volumes; see C. A. Nallino, *Rendic. della R. Academia Naz. dei Lincei* Vol. VII, 1931, p. 342.

IV

THE PINACOTECA

The cardinal also had the liveliest interest in art. He himself told how, while still a boy, he was so taken by a beautiful picture he saw in the house of his cousin Charles, the archbishop of Milan, that he asked him for it as a gift. He was not discouraged by the reaction and eventually to his great joy the picture was given to him. During his years in Rome he loved to visit the catacombs and see there the development of primitive Christian pictures. He was a patron of artists in Rome and housed several of them in his home near the Vatican and later near the Piazza Navona, among them the Flemish artist Joseph Breugel of Velours, who lived in Rome from 1593 to 1595, along with Paul Brill and Joseph Rottenhammer. In Milan he continued this practise of protecting and helping artists: in his villa at Senago for example he was host for a long time to Camillo Procaccini. Cardinal Borromeo contributed to the foundation of the Academy of Drawing, Painting, Sculpture and Architecture in Rome in 1593; afterwards called the Academy of San Luca, and was the first cardinal protector of it, aiding with Federico Zuccari's help the initial growth.

In Milan too, after opening his library, Federico thought immediately of integrating the written patrimony with a gallery of works of art. Borromeo especially wanted to give young people a chance to see and study great models, the works of the best artists. With this in view, he had for years collected pictures and original drawings and had good copies made of other masterpieces. "Knowledge," he wrote in the treatise *Pallas Compta*, "can exist unclothed and nude, but it is better when adorned, much as the beauty of young women is not hidden but enhanced by jewels and gold." He wanted to open a school of painting, sculpture,and architecture in Milan which would promote in a practical way the reforms imposed by the Council of Trent with regard to the use of art in divine worship. Frequent visits to the churches of his diocese put him in touch with the need for providing better decoration of sacred places.

In 1613, Cardinal Federico asked Ludovico Carracci, through Galeazzo Paleotti, nephew of Cardinal Gabriele, Archbishop of Bologna, for the regulations of the Academy of Pictures in Bologna. There was need of new rooms for a school of art or academy. At the same time, it would have to be dependent on the already functioning library. To get the Oblates of San Sepolcro or the Dominicans of Santa Maria della Rosa to leave their houses, already insufficient for them, was impossible so Cardinal Federico turned to the owners of schools founded by Stefano Taverna and offered in exchange for their classrooms and the residence of their teachers a larger house of his own situated in the Via Santa Maria Fulcorina. Having thus obtained the necessary space, Cardinal Federico had the old buildings razed and commissioned a young architect, Fabio Mangone, to construct two large rooms. The new construction was completed between 1611 and 1620 and was separated from the library on the southern side by a small garden. Federico's second building, as we shall see, would be incorporated into Moraglia's new facade in 1831-36. In one of the new rooms, now called the Sala Fagnani, were located statues and gesso work; it was called the *Galleria delle Statue*. In the other, now called the *Sala Custodi*, were placed paintings and drawings and it was called *Galleria delle Pitture*. The two places were probably constructed at different times since the vault of the Fagnani is much higher than that of the Custodi.

In an act notarized April 28, 1618, extending, renewing and executing the munificent codicils already written in 1607 and 1611, Cardinal Federico made a gift of his paintings and drawings to his beloved Ambrosian Library, laying the foundation and forming the nucleus of the Pinacoteca.

The official beginning of the Academy dates from an act notarized June 28, 1625, but already in 1620 Cardinal Federico had printed the governing regulations for such a school of art: *Leges observandae in Academia quae de graphide erit*. Students were to be no older than twenty-four; masters were to be men expert in their art and also capable of discussing and teaching it. Among the first were the painter Giovanni Battista Crespi, called Cerano, the sculptor Andrea Biffi and the architects Carlo Buzzi and Fabio Mangone. The receipt *"in deposito"* of "two charcoal drawings of Raphaele d'Urbino", that the owner, Count Fabio Borromeo, Viscount of Brebbia, agreed to lend Cardinal Federico, is dated July 1, 1610. When Count Fabio died in 1625, his widow, Donna Bianca Spinola, sold "two paintings by Raphael" to Cardinal Federico for the sum of six hundred Imperial Lire on November 23, 1625. It was thus that the cartoons for The School of Athens, which Raphael painted in 1510-1511 for the *Stanza della Segnatura* in the Vatican, became a permanent and conspicuous part of the Pinocateca Ambrosiana.

Borromeo continued to acquire paintings, drawings and books to the last years of his life. The historian Ripamonti wrote that, after the disastrous plague of 1630, the cardinal busied himself saving famous paintings in deserted houses and acquired many of them. This persistent fervor on the part of the cardinal to increase the holdings is much more remarkable when we learn of his profound disappointment with the Ambrosiana and its staff. First of all, it is clear from his correspondence with Antonio Olgiato, the first Prefect, that the founder was too impatient for quick results, that is, for publications by his Scholars. In 1617, when the first volume of Ripamonti's *Historia Ecclesiae Mediolanensis* appeared to much praise, there was also criticism from various important people who claimed they had been maligned in the book. From a distance of three centuries we can recognize that Giuseppe Ripamonti was the most intelligent of the Scholars of the 17th Century and that he knew how to write. Manzoni revived the memory of this historian and praised him in *I Promessi Sposi*, borrowing from him the most salient episodes in the novel. But Ripamonti was a quarrelsome sort who had a sharp tongue and consequently many enemies. They discovered errors in Ripamonti's book and falsely accused him of having used spurious letters of Gregory the Great. He was fair game because they thought him guilty of materialism and atheism: why, once he said a Monsignor at the cathedral was dead as a dodo. Things reached such a point that the Archbishop had to agree to the imprisonment of this Ambrosiana Scholar whom he himself had appointed and to initiate a trial which lasted four years. Someone said that, although Federico did indeed keep Ripamonti in prison for four years, he saved him from the clutches of the Roman Inquisition. Others criticized the cardinal, accusing him of timidity. But Borromeo had his reasons, as can be seen in a letter of March 28, 1619 to his Roman agent, Besozzi, in which, speaking of Ripamonti, he said, "safety alone should be considered lest he give us reason to regret everything." We dwell on this painful incident here only to show that in the 17th Century too promoting culture had its risks.

Federico exhausted his inheritance in order to found the Ambrosiana. He clearly meant it as a work of benevolence: man does not live by bread alone. His intention is shown in his other vast and continuous acts of liberality toward the needy. Manzoni in dramatic episodes of Chapter XXII of *I Promessi Sposi* presents this aspect of the second Borromeo: "his life was a continuous outpouring to the poor." The *Relatione* written in Rome in 1598-99, already cited above, reports that Cardinal Borromeo, despite the large sums he inherited "was never out of debt though his household was modest and his personal life parsimonious. It is thought that his expenses consisted of large secret gifts made particularly through the priests of Vallicella." His generosity during the famine and plague in Milan is well known. Less known is his interest in and aid for the Swiss churches sacked by heretics, and for the hospital built in the Gottardo Pass. Having enlarged it at his own expense, he named a chaplain with a perpetual stipend to minister to those who had to travel through that dangerous pass.

Shadows in the biography of Cardinal Federico are not lacking, as Paolo Bellezza showed in his book of 1931. Cardinal Federico was guilty of exaggerated moralistic criticism of Dante and Petrarch; he took for true the most incredible stories of the naturalists of his time; he saw devils and deviltry everywhere; he shared the worst beliefs of his contemporaries concerning witches, but he does not seem himself to have burned any, though probably he could not have prevented it. Manzoni's praise of him in *Gli Sposi Promessi* ends thus: "he was truly a great man, insofar as so magnificent an epithet can go with such a miserable substantive." The space given to Borromeo in *I Promessi Sposi* is slightly less, but the substance of the praise is kept, and the story of the Ambrosiana as a lively proof of the gentleness, wisdom and grandeur of soul of Federico Borromeo.

NOTES

On Federico's relations with Italian and foreign artists in Rome, see G. Gabrieli, *op. cit.*, 213 ff. ---The original of the donation of 1618 is in the Archivo di Stato di Milano Fondo Notarile: Cancell. Arciv. Civile, Filza 138, fasc. 39. See *Catalogo della Mostra documentaria dell' Arch. di Stato di Milano*, published by Adele Bellu, Milan, 1967, p. 111. ---On the history of Raffaello's cartoon, see L. Beltrami, Il Cartone di Raffaello Sanzio per la 'Scuola d' Atene', Milan, 1919 and K. Oberhuber-L. Vitali, *Il Cartone di Raffaello*, Silvana Editoriale, 1972. ---The imprisonment and trial of Ripamonti are recounted by Francesco Cusani in the introduction to Ripamonti's *La Peste di Milano del 1630, translated by Cusani, Milan, 1841; the letter of March 28, 1619 is discussed there. ---The Academy founded by Federico died along with many other things during the grievous plague of 1630; it was reopened in 1669 to a languid and fitful life; the coup de grace* was administered when the *Accademia Governativa di Belle Arti* was founded at Brera in 1776; see Ceruti, *La Biblioteca Ambrosiana*, Milan, 1880, pp. 97-111. ---On the shadows in the life of Cardinal Federico, see P. Bellezza, *op. cit.*, pp. 58-60 and 129-141 as well as G. Gabrieli, *op. cit*, p. 176 and p. 199.

V

THE AMBROSIANA IN THE 17TH CENTURY

The Ambrosiana, open to everyone, quickly became, after the Duomo, the most conspicuous attraction in Milan, particularly for foreign visitors. The Belgian Errijk De Put (latinized as Ericius Puteanus), professor first at Milan and then at Louvain, in his *Suada Attica*, published in Belgium in 1615, spoke with high praise of the Ambrosiana and its founder and boasted of having been consulted in its foundation. The Dutchman Phillip Wannemaecker had already published his faint praise in 1611. Henry II of Borbone, Prince of Conde, visited the Ambrosiana in 1622 and found it very beautiful. Gabriel Naude, a young Frenchman, named at the age of twenty personal librarian to President De Mesmes, came to Italy in 1626 and waxed enthusiastic over the Ambrosiana: "... so far as I now know, the only (libraries) where one can enter freely and without difficulty are those of Sir Bodley at Oxford, of Cardinal Borromeo at Milan and the House of the Augustinians in Rome; all the others, those of Muret, Fulvius Ursinus, Montalte and the Vatican, as well as the Medici, the Peter Victor at Florence, the Bessarion at Venice, St. Anthony at Padua, the Jacobins at Boulogne, that of the Augustinians at Cremona, Cardinal Siripand's at Naples, Duke Frederick's at Urbain, Nunnesius' at Barcelona, Ximenes' at

Complute, Renzouius' at Bradenberk, Foulcres' at Ausbourg, and finally the King's, the St. Victor and the M. de T. at Paris, which are all beautiful and admirable, are not so public, open to everyone and easy to get into as the three first. For, to speak only of the Ambrosiana in Milan, and to show at the same time how it far surpasses in grandeur and magnificence as well as in catering to the public those in Rome, is it not extraordinary that anyone can enter there at almost any time he likes and stay as long as he pleases, to look, read, take out whatever author he fancies and have all the means and facilities to do so, either in public or private, and with no trouble beyond going there the appropriate days and times, sit in chairs provided for the purpose and ask for the books he wishes to study from the Librarian or his three helpers who are well provided for and paid both to take care of the library and those who come each day to study there?" (pp. 154-156)

This passage from Naude's *Advis pour dresser une bibliotheque*, published in Paris in 1627, gave enormous publicity to the Milanese library. It had two French editions (1627 and 1644); a Latin translation was published in Germany in 1658 and an English translation in 1661, the last reproduced in Cambridge in 1903.

The Marchese Galeazzo Arconati, in an instrument drawn up on January 22, 1637, gave to the Ambrosiana Library twelve Leonardo da Vinci manuscripts, among them the famous *Codice Atlantico*. It was an act of royal munificence. The first visitor to speak of the huge book with the drawings of Leonardo was the Englishman John Evelyn who came to Milan in May 1646. His diary was republished in Oxford by E. S. De Beer in 1955. Eritreo, in his *Pinacotheca*, printed in Cologne in 1643, devotes three pages to the Ambrosiana. Cardinal Guido Bentivoglio of Ferrara, who lived for many years in Flanders and in Paris as representative of the Roman Pontiff, in his *Memorie* published in Venice and Amsterdam in 1648, has a beautiful passage on Cardinal Federico whom he knew in Rome in 1597-1601; he draws a picture of him full of affectionate sympathy. He is not silent on the criticism made of Borromeo's many publications which "did not enjoy great popularity or praise, it being thought that in his Latin works the labors of others were mixed with his own while his vernacular books were judged to be full of affected Tuscanisms, too many ancient and recondite words, and wanting in warm and lively ideas. In any case, of all the patrons and

professors of letters he deserves the highest praise, both for his personal achievements and for having founded the famous Ambrosiana Library in Milan where all the disciplines and sciences are fostered. It is today, because of its particular circumstances, considered the most famous and celebrated in the whole of Europe."

John Henry Pflaumern, in the second edition of his *Mercurius Italicus*, published at Augsburg in 1650, also devotes a page to the Ambrosiana.

In the first half of the 17th Century in many European cities there were collections of various curious objects or "marvels." These where the first museums. Thus, at Naples, the Museo of Ferrante Imperato, at Rome that of Athanasius Kircher near the Collegio Romano, the Cospiano Museum of Bologna, Ole Wurm's museum in Copenhagen and later (1683) the Ashmolean Museum at Oxford. In Milan, a whimsical mathematician, traveler and student of the natural and mechanical sciences, Manfredo Settala (1600-1680) gathered in the rooms of his house on Via Pantano "the most beautiful marvels of nature and art." The Settaliana Collection soon was the object of repeated visits by Milanese and by foreigners when they came to Milan: businessmen and students, magistrates and soldiers, princes, prelates and sovereigns, the last lavishing gifts and honoraria on Settala, thus enabling him to increase his collection. A kind of catalogue was published in Latin by Paolo Terzaghi in 1664 and then a Italian translation by P. F. Scarabelli in 1666, which was reprinted in 1677. A catalogue illustrated with a hundred watercolors is among the Ambrosiana manuscripts. Such a museum can be called an Encyclopedia of Things and it enjoyed fame throughout Europe. It had a series of embalmed esoteric animals, skeltons of rare birds and fish, shells, crustaceans, amber, coral; wild fruits, crystal, hard rocks, fossils; scientific instruments, clocks, lenses, burning mirrors, telescopes, astrolabes, an artistic saddle of decorated metal and other works of art; 9200 volumes, 1600 manuscripts, as well as pictures, medals, coins. In its main lines the Settala Museum is serious and systematic, though it includes strange things, some childish and silly. But it is a good reflection of the 17th Century and of the Baroque. In his will dated July 30, 1672, Manfredo Settala stated that at his death his museum should go to his brother Carlo, bishop of Tortona and, when he died, to his nephews. Should the line be extinguished, the will directed that the museum should be given to the Biblioteca Ambrosiana.

Several pages devoted to the Ambrosiana can be found in Richard Lassels' *Voyage of Italy*, published in London in 1670 and translated into French the following year (*Voyage d'Italie*, Paris, 1671). Lassels wrote, "*The Bibliotheca Ambrosiana is one of the best libraries in Italy, because it is not so coy as the others, which scarse let themselves be seen; whereas this opens its dores publickly to all comers and goers, and suffers Them to read what book they please .... Ouer the heads of the highest shelues, are set up the pictures of learned men, a thing of more cost, then profit; seeing with that cost many more books might have been bought, and learned men are best seen in their books and writings. Loquere, ut te videam.*" (pp. 123-4)

The first history of the Ambrosiana appeared in 1672, *De origine et statu Bibliothecae Ambrosianae Hemidecas*, written by the third Prefect, Pier Paolo Bosca. In one hundred and eighty pages of heavy and obscure Latin, Bosca described the first foundations and the succeeding undertakings of Federico's institution. While not great, Bosca's book remains valuable, not least because of the beautiful plates which give us an idea of the primitive Ambrosiana: it was reprinted by Grevio of Leiden in 1722 in the sixth part of volume nine of his *Thesaurus Antiquitatum et Historiarum Italiae*. There are however serious lacunae in Bosca; for example, he knew nothing of Bentivoglio or Naude.

Carlo Torre's *Portrait of Milan*, published in 1674, devoted five whole pages to the "infinite marvels" of the Ambrosiana.

The greatest scholar of France, Jean Mabillon, visited the Ambrosiana at the end of April, 1685, and stayed fifteen days. He and his traveling companion made a great impression on the Ambrosiana staff by the tireless assiduousness with which they ransacked codices and found many precious things. In the first volume of his *Iter Italicum Litterarium* (Paris, 1687), Mabillon did not fail to praise the riches of the Ambrosiana.

The same year, 1685, the Anglican prelate Gilbert Burnet, who was then preparing his history of the reform of the English church, visited the Ambrosiana. In his letters, published in Amsterdam in 1686, he recalls the people he had seen crowding Federico's large hall, and the convenience of pen, ink and paper on each desk at the disposition of anyone wishing to take notes. He laments the fact that he did not find manuscripts of the works of St. Ambrose, particularly that of the *De Sacramentis*. Actually there are many such manuscripts in the Ambrosiana. Burnet, like many other visitors, wanted to find everything at once.

Francis Maximilian Misson, French politician and literary man who had emigrated to London, came to Milan in 1688. After admiring the picturesque collection of the Settala Museum at the Porta Romana, he came to the Ambrosiana. He felt that the claim of twelve thousand manuscripts and seventy two thousand printed volumes was exaggerated and judged there were at most forty thousand volumes in all. He noted with pleasure that provisions had been made for heating in winter as in the Benedictine library of St. Victor in Paris. The Geschwindsche Library in Vienna was also heated. These three were at the time the only public libraries with heating. He admired at length the pictures in the gallery, especially the Bruegels.

NOTES

The visit of the Prince of Conde is recounted in *Voyage en Italie de M. le Prince de Conde*, Lyon, 1666, p. 14. ---The university library of Oxford, founded in 1327, was restored, renovated, provided with funds and opened to the public by Sir Thomas Bodley November 8, 1602. Fr. Milkau in his *Handbuchder Bibliothekswissenschaft*, Zweite Aufl. von G. Leyh, III, Wiesbaden, 1955, pp. 298-300, says, "Man hat die Bibliotheca Ambrosiana das katholische Gegenstuck zur Bodleiana genannt, denn was die Schopfung Thomas Bodleys in Oxford fur die englische Gelehrnwelt bedeutete, das sollte nach dem Willen des Federico Borromeo fur Italien die von ihm begrundete Bibliothek werden." ---Certain rules that Bodley established for the Bodleian are found in Federico's for the Biblioteca Ambrosiana; it is noteworthy that in his house in Rome Cardinal Borromeo had as master of theology an exiled Englishman, Daniel Halsworth. ---The third library praised by Naude, that of the *Maison des Augustins* is the *Angelica*, the first public Roman library, which was opened a few years after the Ambrosiana. ---On John Evelyn, see *The Diary of John Evelyn* by E. S. de Beer, II, Oxford, 1955, p. 497 ff. ---On Bentivoglio's eulogy, see his *Memorie e Lettere*. Bari, 1934, pp. 52-53. ---On the first museums, see G. Bazin, *The Museum Age*, Brussels, 1967; on Settala and his museum, see G. Fogolari in *Arch. Stor. Lomb.* XXVII, Milan, 1900, pp. 58-126, and C. Tavernari, "*Il Museo Settala 1660-1680*," in *Critica d'Arte*, n. I63-I65, Florence, 1979, pp. 202-220. ---F. M. Misson, *Nouveau Voyage d'Italie fait en l'annee 1688,* Seconde partie, at the Hague, 1691, p. I93 ff.

VI

MURATORI

At the end of 1694, the Benedictine B. Bacchini recommended to Counts Carlo and Giberto Borromeo that they take on as a Doctor of the Ambrosiana his twenty-two year old pupil, Ludovico Antonio Muratori. The young man arrived in Milan and entered the Ambrosiana in the beginning of February, 1695. At last the library had a librarian worthy of the treasures Federico had collected at such great expense. The letters that young Muratori wrote to his friends in Modena during those first days in Milan are amusing, but they also contain serious criticisms. As for the Ambrosiana, he felt that "neither the quality of the books nor their arrangement pleases since none of the many systems of making libraries convenient and beautiful is used. Everything is confused, very confused, aimed rather to please the eye than anything else. *Bertoldini* (that is, comic papers, strip cartoons) or the next thing to them, we have by the thousands, but of good modern books we are in want, although with every year more are being bought. But one can study here and I would not for these reasons abandon the opportunity." The pay was not splendid ("ten Filippi a month more or less"), but the Borromeos gave him hope of greater things. "The job is most attractive, entailing nothing but study. The task will be to publish a book every three years, but the custom is not yet established. Two hours in the morning and two more after dinner in residence, though that is not my whole obligation. With holidays and vacations, I will have half the year to myself ..."

Delightful scenes are captured. "The library is a lovely place, somewhat like a church, really, and one good fellow came in and genuflected, thinking himself in a place of worship, then looked around for an altar and chapel and realized it had been dechurched. Seats are scattered about as well as stands to hold the reader's books. At times there are a hundred people here .... We three Doctors are seated majestically at tables on big chairs with three servants at our and the other readers disposal. Nobility and foreigners come in often to look at everything, which is courteously shown them; I wish no entanglements and am not obliged to do this sort of thing. But I think that if your dear heart [the beloved of his friend Tori in Modena] should show up here you would willingly forego study for a chance to wait on a lady who is most certainly beautiful ...." He worked with passion and tenacity. In 1697 appeared his first volume of hitherto unedited materials from Ambrosiana codices; the second volume appeared in 1698. Both are publications still worthwhile and useful today.

Muratori must have read an incredible number of codices during the five years he stayed in Milan. The so-called "Muratori Fragment" could not have been found by chance: he made it known in 1740 when his name was already celebrated throughout Europe for the publication of the twenty-seven folio volumes of the *Rerum Italicarum Scriptores*. But he had it in custody for forty years. Thus when in 1706 he published the treatise *Della perfetta poesia*, he recalled a codex he had seen in the Ambrosiana, in which he had recognized in some anonymous Spanish verses the hand of Pietro Bembo.

Far beyond his work on particular codices, Muratori, in his five years at the Ambrosiana, conceived and developed the idea of publishing the medieval sources of the history of the Italian people, formed from the fusion of German invaders with various Latin peoples. This project found very energetic and enthusiastic support in Milan, so much so that in thirty years it was brought to a superb conclusion.

Manzoni, better than anyone else, celebrated the greatness of Muratori in his *Discorso sulla Storia Longobardica* of 1822, in the words Giosue Carducci selected for quotation in his 1900 preface to the first volume of the new edition of the *Rerum Italicarum Scriptores*. This greatness and renown reflected on Federico's institution, from which Muratori appeared to have emerged.

Nonetheless he had his complaints about the Ambrosiana. We have already mentioned the letter in which he speaks of the *Bertoldini*. Elsewhere he deplores the fact that the collection of manuscripts "is without a catalogue, the whole thing confused." In June, 1698, he wrote to Magliabechi, "I am full of fury because I don't have certain books I need...Although our library has many books, I do not find the best ones there, because it lacks many of the latest."

The learned Bernard de Montfaucon, who had already been in correspondence with Muratori, came from Paris in June of 1698 to see the Ambrosiana manuscripts. In ten pages of his *Diarium Italicum* (Paris, 1702), he would publish the first list of the more important Ambrosiana codices. Montfaucon adopted Muratori's complaints: "Although the Ambrosiana library comprises forty thousand books, it nonetheless lacks many extremely necessary ones as well as the more accurate editions of the Fathers."

Another great difficulty was the pedantry with which the *Conservatori* interpreted the article of Federico's Constitution prohibiting codices to be copied. In February, 1698, Muratori wrote to Arisi, "with respect to the treatises of Salerno, I must tell you that when I requested permission of the *Conservatori* to make copies of them, they denied it to me on the grounds that it would be a clear violation of the wishes of our founder the Lord Cardinal." In May, 1699, he wrote to Apostolo Zeno, "I lament my lack of luck and regret the rules of this library. Cardinal Federico Borromeo its founder left explicit printed orders that only a fragment of any manuscript could be copied. This is known to Mr. Rostgaard and the Benedictine fathers and a thousand others who come here every day and I have been unable to persuade to the contrary the Congregation supervising this place, all of whom say that a book copied no longer belongs to the library. The fame which would come to the place, the usefulness for the learned, and many other arguments go unheard and I, to my sorrow, cannot comply with the requests of other friends who have similar plans ...."

Despite his disappointment over the paucity of modern books and his annoyance at the impenetrable obtuseness of the *Conservatori*, when Muratori left Milan on August 10, 1700 for Modena and the post of archivist of Rinaldo d'Este, he "felt heavy sorrow and singular tenderness" at having to leave "the most gentle heaven of Milan." "I will never be able to forget the Ambrosiana," he wrote Magliabechi on August 30, 1700, "and the great convenience for my studies I experienced there."

Muratori left a profound mark on the Ambrosiana; he was an effective model for colleagues and successors, and the library began to be a cultural center for scholars throughout Europe. It was in Muratori's time that correspondence began with the Bollandists Papebroch and Janninck and with erudite men of France, Holland and Germany.

The two great prefects of the 18th Century, Giuseppe Antonio Sassi (1711-1751) and Baldassarre Oltrocchi (1767-1797) can be called emulators of Muratori and worthy continuers of his tradition. Sassi, author among other things of a history of printing in Milan, in 1747 also succeeded in starting up again the Ambrosiana press which had been closed for a century.

18th Century Milan, the cheeky ladykillers of its public places aside, was a place of solidity, industry, study. And the Ambrosiana played the chief role in the area of study. Illustrious visitors were, in 1701, the English politician and essayist J. Addison; in 1707 the Seigneur of Blainville; in 1714 the Count of

Caylus; in 1728 Montesquieu who observed of the Ambrosiana that it "est extremement bien tenue;" in 1729 the historian J. G. Keyssler; in 1730 the famous professor of physics, Christian Gabriel Fischer, came, exiled from Koenigsberg. Serviliano Latuada, in the fourth volume of his *Descrizione di Milano*, which appeared in 1728, gave a full account of the Ambrosiana library and gallery: it was carefully written by the Prefect G. A. Sassi at the request of the King of Portugal. Among personalities visiting the Ambrosiana in 1739 were Lady Mary Montagu Worthley and the president of the Dijon parliament, Charles de Brosses. The latter's account of his visit mentions the skeleton of a beautiful *femme docteur* who had in her will left her bones for research. Most likely this was a skeleton used by students in the Academy and their story an imaginative explanation of it. Goethe's father visited in 1740.

The Settala Museum became part of the Ambrosiana collection in 1751 after a lengthy legal battle; a decision of the Milan Senate on February 19 went against its last unlawful possessor: "The Settala Gallery and the things which make it up should go to the College of the Ambrosiana Library." Serious losses and damage to the Settala collection had been suffered in 1680 when its founder died and the bulk of the contents of the museum were used to decorate the catafalque and the long cortege. There were certainly other losses in subsequent decades since we possess written complaints by the *Conservatori* of the Ambrosiana at the many and noteworthy discrepancies between the inventory in the will and the inventory of the consignment. At the time there was no free space for the Settala Museum and the collection had to be dispersed and distributed in several rooms.

NOTES

The letter concerning the *Bertoldini* is dated March 2, 1695; see M. Campori, *Epistolario di L. A Muratori*, I, Modena, 1901, p. 75; the story of the genuflecting visitor is in a letter of March 23, 1695: Campori, I, p. 179; the lament on the catalogues is in Campori, I., p. 324; the letter to Arisi in Campori, I, p. 299 and that to Apostolo Zeno in Campori, II, p. 395; the letter of August 1700 to Magliabechi in Campori, II, p. 457. ---For Jóhn Addison's visit, see his *Remarks on Several Parts of Italy*, London, 1705, p. 34. ---Montesquieu's visit: A. Montesquieu, *Voyages de Montesquieu*, I, Bordeaux, 1894, p. 92. ----C. G. Fischer's observations were published by A. Predeek, "Bibliotheksbesuche eines gelehrten Reisenden im Anfange des 18 Jahrh.," in *Zentralbl. f. Bibliothekswesen*, 45, 1928, pp. 346 ff. ---On Lady Montagu's visit, see *Arch. St. Lomb.*,1906, II, p. 251 and for that of de Brosses *Lettres historiques et critiques sur l'Italie de Charles de Brosses*, I, Paris, 1799, p. 121 ff. ---Goethe's father: see J. C. Goethe, *Viaggio in Italia*, I. Rome, I932, p. 368. ---On Oltrocchi, see S. Ritter, *Baldassarre Oltrochhi e le sue memorie storichesu lavita di Leonardo da Vinci*, Rome, 1925.

VII

THE LATTER PART OF THE 18TH CENTURY AND THE FRENCH REQUISITIONS

The famous historian Edward Gibbon visited the Ambrosiana on May 15, 1764 and was the first to note the items from the Settala Museum in their new location. The eighteen year old Vittorio Alfieri was still a dissolute youth in 1766 when he began his Italian journey. In the Ambrosiana Library he was shown the Petrarch autograph: "I threw it away saying it would mean nothing to me."

Charles Burney the Englishman came to see the musical codices of the Ambrosiana in July, 1770. Oltrocchi the Prefect showed him the Bobbio missal of the 10th Century with musical notation *in campo aperto*. The Marchese don Carlo Trivulzio, founder of the Trivulziana Library, was presented to Burney in the reading room.

At the end of 1767, G. B. Branca, a Scholar of the Ambrosiana, informed various foreign scholars of the famous Syro-Hexaplaris biblical codex. J. J. Bjornstahl, the Swede, came to see it in 1773, studied it at length, and transcribed various portions of it. Another Swede, M. Norberg, arrived in Milan in 1778 to continue the study of this codex begun by Bjornstahl and would later complain of the Ambrosiana librarians. But there must have been discourtesy on Norberg's side too, as we learn from Andres; Antonio Ceriani, in the preface to his photoprinted edition of the codex, makes mention of the merits of Branca and his courtesies toward the Swedish scholars.

Juan Andres published a full narrative of his 1791 visit to the Ambrosiana in the fourth volume of his *Cartes Familiares* (Madrid, 1793). In a curious anonymous volume, which must be by Norberto Caimi, printed in 1778, probably in Milan, and entitled *L'Italia*, many books and manuscripts of the Ambrosiana ("which alone would suffice to clear the densest minds in Milan") are mentioned. A Roman lady, the Marchesa Margherita Boccapadule Sparapani Gentili, who came to visit Milan in 1794 with her friend Alessandro Verri rightly complained of the confusion in the Ambrosiana art collections. The English writer John Moore, in the account of his Italian trip published in London in 1781, recounts the story of the woman's skeleton, no longer that of a *dottoressa*, but of a beauty.

On May 15, 1796 Napoleon triumphally entered a joyful Milan grandly illuminated for the occasion. Three days later new taxes squelched the joy. The Lombard provinces were required to pay immediately an extraordinary tax of twenty million. Clouds formed above the Ambrosiana as well. The library and gallery attracted the not disinterested attention of the invaders. "Agents of the Sciences and Fine Arts of the National Academy of Paris attached to the Army in Italy" came to the Ambrosiana May 19, June 10 and 25, 1796, requisitioned and took away twelve paintings, some twenty drawings, nineteen manuscripts, a dozen incunabula and six assorted pieces. Gaetano Bugati, the pro-prefect, made a careful list of all these things. The list, dated December 27, 1797, was published by Achille Ratti in 1907. As has already been mentioned, twelve Leonardo de Vinci manuscripts, a Rubens painting, another by Giorgione, various drawings and several incunabula, would not be returned from Paris in 1815.

In 1796 Oltrocchi, then 82 years old, was still Prefect of the Ambrosiana. Complaints reached the ministers of the Cisalpine Republic who had to provide for the Ambrosiana. Oltrocchi died in November, 1797 and G. B. Branca, himself seventy-five, succeeded him. These were years of continual anguish for those at the Ambrosiana as well as for other good people in a city where executions took place for obscure reasons, making them think the *liberte* come from France was a tragic mask. The proximity of the library to the motherhouse of the Oblates led to the mistaken notion in governing circles that the Ambrosiana

Doctors were dependents of the Oblates who were thought to be dangerous reactionaries absolutely hostile to the new government. In December 1787 the Emperor Joseph II had put the Dominicans out of the little church of Santa Maria della Rosa and given it to the Oblates. In March 1798 the Oblates in their turn were expelled from the church. The Cisalpine governor intended to use the deconsecrated church as the seat of the Constitutional Circle, an offshoot of the *Societa Popolare Patriottica*, formed by a fanatic group of anticlerical extremists. Two steps from the Ambrosiana demonstrations were held daily inciting to the destruction and overturning of temples of "superstition." Cusani recounts that one night the youngest daughter of Paolo Sangiorgio, a citizen and professor of chemistry, concluded her inflamed mouthings against religion by offering herself in marriage to whomever would bring her the head of Pope Pius VI, "the pretended head of the Catholic imposture." By a happy accident in October 1798 the vault of the little old church (it was constructed between 1480 and 1493) caved in and the notorious *Circolo* had to move, to the great relief of the librarians.

In April, 1801, a lenghty report from the Prefect of the Archives, Luigi Bossi, proposed the nationalization of the Ambrosiana. A solution was suggested for the College of Doctors; better pay and maintenance was forseen for the custodian, Cesare della Croce, and the two scribes, Perego and Mazzucchelli, most helpful because of their knowledge of ancient and modern languages.

This report, published a few years ago by Giovanni Vittani, provides much interesting information about the condition of the library in those years. Many of the complaints set forth in the Bossi report will seem strange, some inconsistent, but others are not lacking in foundation: "There is an infinite number of holidays in the course of the year ... reading hours are extremely brief ...." Something similar had been said by Muratori a hundred years before. "The multitude of holidays is one of the public complaints; so too perhaps the rudeness of the servants who do not go graciously in search of books, often reply that the book is not there without checking it in the index and no sooner is the brief two hours of opening past than they rudely impound the books and cut off on the spot the working of the readers. And there continues at the same library the most despicable abuse of refusing any book inscribed on the index of prohibited books in Rome unless the requester can produce a letter of permission equally Roman ...."

The Bossi report was sent in secret by Minister Pancaldi to the National Counsel Crespi for an opinion. Luckily Crespi delayed his reply until the end of September. At the end of August 1801 the Minister Pancaldi was informed that in Paris, confronted by the dispatches from the Cisalpine Republic, Bonaparte had "inveighed in general against all measures which would attack religion or property; he said...that it was necessary to respect the priests, and at once put aside this revolutionary conduct and let all citizens live in peace...that if the system was not changed, he would be the first to abandon us here to our fate."

It was understood in high places in Milan that the time of fury had passed. Crespi's favorable view of the Bossi Report was put aside and the autonomy of the Ambrosiana was saved.

In those days Ugo Foscolo also complained of too many holidays: "these Ambrosiana and national (that is, of the library of Brera) librarians enjoy more holidays and vacations than befit men of letters and their aides."

A decree published by Napoleon April 25, 1810, ordered the suppression of all religious orders. The Oblate Fathers of Milan would have to leave diocesan seminaries, the college of Gorla Minore and even the house of San Sepolcro. The administrators of the Ambrosiana, fearing to see the house of the suppressed Oblates become the property of some who wanted it and, on the other hand, wishing to get rid of unsavory neighbors, had recourse, with the interposition of Count Giberto Borromeo, Perpetual Trustee, to the Minister of the Interior, Vaccari, and then to the Minister of Finance of the Italian Kingdom, Prina. They thus obtained the right to acquire as the result of negotiation "the place, that is, the college of the suppressed Oblates of Milan, excluding the church, declared succursale, and the place that the official expert declared necessary for the housing of the coadjutors who must remain for the service of the church." For the sum of 44,188.12 lire living quarters for the Prefect of the library and the procurator were acquired and two oratories, earlier in service of the church, that of the *Guardian Angel* (now the *Sala Stocchetti*) and *delle Dame* (now called the *Sala Luini*) which were used for housing books. It was also possible to provide new surroundings for the meetings of the Trustees (the *Sala del Consiglio* which in 1924 because the Prefect's room). This was the first addition to the buildings of the Ambrosiana after two centuries of existence. One can consult the plan drawn up in 1922 by the architect Ambrogio Annoni.

NOTES

Edward Gibbon's *Journey from Geneva to Rome* is edited by G. A. Bonnard, London, 1961; see pp. 50-52. ---V. Alfieri, *La Vita*, edited by L. Negri, Turin, 1921, p. 155. ---C. Burney, *The Present State of Music in France and Italy*, I, London, 1773, p. 112. ---A. Ceriani, *Codex Syro-Hexaplaris Ambrosianus Photolithographice editus*, Milan, 1874. ---The critique of the Marchesa Boccapadule can be found in *Arch. St. Lomb.*, 1917, p. 358. ---John Moore, *A Riew of Society and Manners in Italy*, II, London, 1795, p. 407. ---Bugati's list is in A. Ratti's *Guidasommaria per il visitatore della Biblioteca Ambrosiana*, Milan, 1907, p. 140. ---Sangiorgio's outbursts are described by G. Galbiati, *Il tempio dei Crociati e degli Oblati*, Milan, 1930, p. 46. ---Bossi's report was published by G. Vittani in *Scritti vari dedicati a Mario Armanni*, Milan, 1938, pp. 251-269. ---On the laments of U. Foscolo, see *Scritti letterari e politici dal 1796 al 1808*, Florence, 1972, p. 446.

VIII

ANGELO MAI

Another Napoleonic decree lay at the origin of the series of accidents which brought Angelo Mai to the Ambrosiana. In July 1806, Joseph Napoleon ordered the expulsion of all foreign religious from Naples. Thus the student Angelo Mai had to leave Naples, since in 1804, at the age of 22, he had donned the Jesuit habit. At the College of Orvieto two Spanish Jesuits taught him both paleography and how to treat palimpsest codices with chemical reagents. In February 1809 another decree of Napoleon ordered that foreign religious were to be expelled from ex-Pontifical territories. Mai with his companion had to leave Orvieto and they came to Milan where he made arrangements to live on odd jobs. During his philosophical studies at Parma Mai had had the opportunity to learn oriental languages at the school of Bernardo De Rossi. It was likely because of this useful knowledge that Mai, in August, 1810, was taken on at the Ambrosiana as "scrittore" for the annual stipend of five hundred lire. The official decision to hire him came on December 16, 1810.

Suddenly in 1811 Mai began to be talked of because of the famous illustrated codex of Homer. Then in 1813 he discovered unedited fragments of the Orations of Cicero. Examining the codex R 57 sup. in the Bobbio collection, on which in the 7th

Century the Easter hymns of Sedulius had been written, Mai saw that the manuscript had been "rewritten," that is, that some folios of the parchment had already been used a first time, in the 5th Century, to inscribe the Orations of Cicero, to be exact. In 1814, in the same troubled months which saw in Milan the massacre of the Minister Prina and the reestablishment of the Austrians, Mai published in a little book of modest aspect several unedited pages of Cicero. The interest this discovery created in the world of scholars, especially foreign ones, was enormous. Codex E 147 sup. is a copy of the acts of the first council of Chalcedon, probably written at Bobbio in the 7th Century. This codex too was "rewritten" and Mai was the first to perceive it and to succeed in reading the primitive writings of the 5th and 6th Centuries. These amount to various things: notes on Cicero, an Arian treatise, discourses of Symmachus, a panegyric of Pliny, letters of Frontone. It was particularly the unedited letters of Frontone, which Mai published in two volumes in 1815, that brought Mai and the Ambrosiana to the attention of many, as if it were a discovery of enormous importance. A century and a half later, reflecting on such clamorous cultural events, one must conclude that Mai had extraordinary luck. Not only to find at his fingertips a good collection of palimpsests in the Bobbio codices, but even more the good fortune of working at a time when the Ambrosiana was frequented by such patrons of antiquity as Count Giberto Borromeo and Count Giacomo Mellerio. These worthies immediately gave Mai the means to print and make known the unedited things he discovered.

Another bit of luck came Mai's way from a direction no one would have imagined. In those years there lived in the obscure town of Recanati on the Adriatic coast a young poet of uncommon genius, who, in enforced solitude from his tenth to his eighteenth year, stubbornly devoted himself to the study of every sort of ancient learning with such fanatical passion that he ruined his health: Giacomo Leopardi. For years he had been eager to publish at least some of his many writings. When in 1815 news came to his uncivilized native town of the Milanese discovery of Frontone, the eighteen year old philological enthusiast felt his heart sink. By chance, a few months before Mai made his discovery, Leopardi had put together with no little labor the fragments of Frontone which could be found in other writers. Leopardi had hardly learned of the Milanese edition of Mai than he immediately set himself the task of making a translation of and commentary on the new texts. He dedicated it to Mai and off the manuscript went to the Milan publisher, Stella. The latter, however, perhaps on the advice of Mai, did not wish to publish the work from Recanati. The admiration of Leopardi might have annoyed Mai; he realized that the young man knew more than he about the meaning of the newly discovered Latin texts. A few years later, at the end of December, 1819, scarcely two months after arriving in Rome, Mai announced the discovery, again in a Bobbio codex that had come to the Vatican Library, of the *De republica* of Cicero. The enthusiasm of Leopardi for the *scopritor famoso* overflowed in the famous canzone "Ad Angelo Mai" written in ten or twelve days in January, 1820. What the poetry of Leopardi meant for Mai's reputation and thence that of the Ambrosiana, can be seen if one recalls that it was in 1816 that the discovery of the *Institutiones* of Gaius was made by Niebuhr in a codex of the capitulary library of Verona, a work at least as important as the *De republica*. But no Leopardi concerned himself with Niebuhr and his name is remembered by no one outside the small circle of philologists and jurists.

The fragments of Plautus were another discovery of Mai in the Ambrosiana codices. And then in 1817 the *Wulfila*. These pages in Gothic, written in the 6th Century in southern Italy, were of enormous interest to the whole Germanic world for the history of the German language. Count Carlo Ottavio Castiglioni (1785-1849) collaborated with Mai in the reading and publication of the fragments of the *Wulfila*.

It should be added that, to make these discoveries, Mai was authorized to use chemical reagents on the Bobbio parchments. Unfortunately, in not a few cases, these caused irreparable damage to the codices. Some criticisms by German philogists of Mai's work were perhaps excessive, -- "Prussian" philologists like F. W. Ritschl and W. Studemund also used chemical reagents on Ambrosiana codices, with ruinous results --- but it is certain that many times he allowed himself to be overcome by haste and impatience. On May 4, 1816, he was named the third Doctor of the Ambrosiana; three years later he was called to the Vatican Library. He left Milan for Rome on October 31, 1819.

Famous visits to the Ambrosiana were more frequent than usual during the Mai years. In 1811 there was the swift passage of Stendahl who visited the Ambrosiana "without pleasure" and found nothing interesting there, but in those months he was completely occupied in romantic liaisons with the beauties of Milan. Despite the disappointing pages of the *Journal d'Italie*, we know that Stendahl frequented the Pinacoteca of the Ambrosiana with some assiduity during the years in which he studied Italian painting. Of his fleeting stay in Milan in June, 1815, when the first confused news of the disaster of Waterloo arrived, Georges Mallet remembered only the Duomo and the Ambrosiana. A. L. Millin, on the other hand, who was the conservator of the cabinet of medals of the king of France, devotes twenty five pages to the Ambrosiana in the first volume of his *Voyage dans le Milanais*, published in Paris in 1817, dwelling in a special way on the discoveries of Mai, whom he sees as bent on transcribing the Bobbio codices.

In 1815 each of the allied powers sent an agent to Paris to get back its own works of art which had been taken off by the French. For Lombardy, the Austrian governor appointed the Baron von Ottenfels, who restored to the Ambrosiana codices which were in the *Bibliotheque Nationale* (the *Codex Atlantico* among them); he did not know that in the library of the *Institut de France* were eleven other Leonardo da Vinci manuscripts which had been taken from the Ambrosiana. These would remain there and never come back, despite the steps taken by Count Giovanni Borromeo, Perpetual Trustee, to obtain their return.

In October, 1816, an English poet, twenty-eight years old and already famous, came to Milan: Lord Byron. He admired the Duomo and La Scala, but in the Ambrosiana he paled with emotion before the lock of blonde hair of Lucrezia Borgia, "more blonde than can be imagined," Byron wrote his friend Murray in a letter of October 16, in which he also laments that he had not been allowed to copy the correspondence between the Duchess of Ferrara and Pietro Bembo. The romantic Lord continued to read and reread those brief amorous missives in order to commit them to memory. In his fanatic admiration he wanted at least one of those hairs. Indeed, in another letter to Murray, he says he keeps that blond strand as a relic: Bernardo Gatti, the Prefect then, published this correspondence in 1859, and wrote that "being a poet, Byron was so crazed that he stole from the library a hair of the Borgia woman."

After Byron, and because of him, that lock of hair acquired an incredible fame, and throughout the 19th Century, Lucrezia Borgia's hair became an object of mandatory admiration and veneration. Even today it is displayed in a precious case designed and made by Alfredo Ravasco in 1934. Is it authentic? The first information on the brief Bembo-Borgia correspondence is given by Muratori, who identified the anonymous lovers. The prefect Oltrocchi published an excellent *Dissertazione* on these letters and poems in 1757 and notes that "at the end of the codex ... is found a fine parchment, folded like an envelope, wrapped in four ribbons, which contains a lock of real hair, blonde, thin and rather long, just the kind Bembo is accustomed to praise so much both in his poems and in the Asolani; and these by constant tradition are thought and always in our memory were thought to be hairs of the aforementioned Borgia." The codex came to the Ambrosiana from the Library of Gian Vincenzo Pinelli. "This was a man who must have found them there and kept them where they were when he came into possession of this manuscript as well as of other things which had belonged to Bembo. The trail thus leads to Bembo himself. Is it imaginable that he would have put the hair of another woman with Lucrezia's letters?" Thus wrote Pio Rajna in his 1914 study. Hair and letters and Spanish poems refer to the third of the youthful loves of Bembo, of whom with boundless vanity he continued into old age to keep writings and souvenirs; in short, to his relations with the Duchess of Ferrara in the years 1502-1502. At the time Lucrezia was twenty-two and lived in Ferrara with her third husband Alfonso d'Este. Contemporaries say that if Lucrezia's life in her first twenty years was discussible, after she became the wife of Alfonso she was irreproachable.

The Ambrosiana codex puts a question mark to that assertion.

Some wished Ravasco's case to be eliminated from the new arrangement of the Pinacoteca, but it was thought wiser to continue to exhibit it: in the first place, to retain something of the Settala type, that is, something of a curiosity-museum sort; in the second place, to enable people to see the object of so much enthusiasm in the romantic age as well as the subject of learned studies. As Luigi Gramatica wrote in a preface found among his letters and published in 1950 by Carlo Dionisotti, "it seems destiny that the most compromising moral documents of Bembo's intimate life should end in the Ambrosian Library in Milan and that the task of explaining them should fall to its librarians."

Sidney Owenson, better known as Lady Morgan, the wife of Thomas Charles Morgan, was already a celebrated writer when she visited the Ambrosiana in 1819. To it she dedicated four pages of her work, *Italy*, published in London and New York in 1921 and in a French translation in Brussels in 1825. She marveled over the precious manuscripts and the autograph of Petrarch relating to the death of Laura and the Leonardo Codex, but above all Lady Morgan could not contemplate too much the figure of Mai buried in his codices, "still in all the first triumph of his new discoveries." Her infatuation for Mai made her see impossible things: the writing desk at which the librarian sits is antique; the light which falls upon his head comes from a narrow

Gothic window, and is reflected on a great cross of gold which shines on his black habit. We would like to know what Mai might have said on reading in Lady Morgan's book that his honest face of a Bergamo mountaineer "in its transparent paleness and strongly-marked features presented one of those splendid originals, which Italy alone supplies to the genius of painting."

NOTES

Mai's activities before coming to Milan and then during his Ambrosiana years are described in G. Gervasoni's, *L'ambiente letterario milanese nel secondo decennio dell'Ottocento*, Fontes Ambrosiana XI, Florence, 1936; see too G. Gervasoni, *Angelo Mai*, Bergamo, 1954, and the first volume of the *Epistolario* of Angelo Mai, Florence, 1954. --On the damage caused by Ritschl and Studemund, cf. *Rheinisches Museum fur Philologie*, 115 B, H.4, 1972, pp. 365-366. --- For the visits of Stendahl, Mallet, Millin and many other illustrious strangers, see G. Morazzoni, *L'Ambrosiana nel terzo centenario di Federico Borromeo*, Milan, 1932, pp. 87-104. ---For Byron's visit and studies of the Borgia locks, see P. Rajna, *I versi Spagnoli di Pietro Bembo e di Lucrezia Borgia serbati da un codice Ambrosiano*, in *Homenaje a Menendez Pidal*, Madrid, 1924, pp. 299-321; Gramatica's preface was published by C. Dionisotti in the volume of Maria Savorgnan-Pietro Bembo, *Carteggio d'amore*, Florence, 1950. Dionisotti published 77 letters from Savorgnan to Bembo which had been found by Gramatica in the Ambrosiana and now are with Gramatica's letters in the Vatican Library (ms. Vat. lat. 14189). -- On the fantasies of Lady Morgan, see her *Italy* I, London, 1821, pp. 88-92.

IX

ALESSANDRO MANZONI

Some thirty years ago Filippo Meda wrote, "Alessandro Manzoni would not have dwelt so long on Federico Borromeo, would not have studied him with so much love, given such a lively portrait of him or presented him in so sympathetic a light, if he had not been worthy of it, if he had not been, that is, a man who in himself and in his work did not have a real claim to celebrity." In Federico, Manzoni sought to present the ideal of a man of the Church. But he held himself to presenting him as he really was, not as he ought to have been. The figure of Cardinal Federico is essential to the construction of the novel *I Promessi Sposi*. The great book is not poetic creation or fantasy alone. Manzoni's heartfelt wish was to show that certain ancient and modern flaws in the Catholic world were and are the infrequent consequences of human weakness, not the necessary fruits of the plant itself. It occurred to him to put forth as a concrete example the grandeur, rectitude, generosity and disinterestedness of a man of the Church, an archbishop. Despite the oblivion into which the name of that archbishop had been allowed to fall, even in his own city, Manzoni is concerned to show that something of this man still lives, something that is great: the Ambrosiana Library. Hence the "quattro parole" (in fact, six or seven pages) that Manzoni devotes to Cardinal Federico and the Ambrosiana in Chapter XXII of the novel. This was not the result of the splendor of Mai's discoveries; Mai's name does not occur even once in the correspondence of Manzoni. To write of Federico and his work, Manzoni must surely have had recourse at times to the Ambrosiana as well, but it is unlikely that he went there often. The people at the Ambrosiana then would not have seemed very attractive to him. Mai was a classicist; his discoveries caused too much stir and could seem somewhat technical matters. If the anonymous 17th Century manuscript whose story Manzoni jokingly said he had stolen was really the *Historia del Cavalier Perduto* published in 1644 by Pace Pasini in Venice, it would then be a certainty that he had seen and read it in the Ambrosiana, the only library in Milan that had it. But this theory put forward by G. Getto has not met with much agreement.

Pio Paschini, in a 1937 article, maintained, as others had, that the portrait of Federico painted by Manzoni in his novel is half-legendary, a picture in which can be seen his friend Antonio Rosmini rather than the 17th Century archbishop. The opinion is of fragile foundation. Rather than the book of Dupront, Paschini could and should have consulted Pastor's many pages on Cardinal Borromeo, the solid biography of Paolo Bellezza which he does not so much as cite, and the thoughtful article of Filippo Meda already mentioned. The greatness of Cardinal Federico was not imagined by Manzoni.

I Promessi Sposi revived the fame of the second Borromeo and for the library proved to be a providential gift. After the novel appeared in Milan (1826-27), the Ambrosiana acquired many new friends, as generous and munificent as the founder.

NOTES

See F. Meda, "Il secondo Borromeo," in *Vita e Pensiero*, Milan, 1931, pp. 17-29. ---On Pasini's novel, see G. Getto in *Lettere Italiane*, XII, Florence, 1960, p. 141 ff. ---P. Paschini's article is in *Dict. d'Hist. et Geogr. Eccl.*,IX, Paris, 1937, col. 1281-1283. The matter is treated more fully in A. Paredi, "Storicita de 'Federigo' manzoniano," in *Vita e Pensiero*, Milan, 1972, pp. 282-291.

X

EXPANSIONS OF 1826-1836

On April 26, 1826, the Conservators of the Ambrosiana renewed their request that they be permitted to acquire the crumbling and abandoned church of Santa Maria della Rosa, which, after the departure of the *Circolo Constituzionale* became in 1804 the workshop of the makers of stage scenery for La Scala. The negotiations were prolonged. Finally, on May 9, 1829, the Austrian governor authorized the Congregazione Municipale to sell about two thirds of the city owned property to the Ambrosiana Library for the price of 78,494 lire, if the municipality of Milan would pay the state 26,691 lire for the rest. Thus the city was able to enlarge somewhat Via San Sepolcro, now called Via Cardinale Federico Borromeo, and to construct the piazza called della Rosa until not many years ago. The little old church, designed, it is said, by Bramante in 1456, began to be razed in 1831. Of its many pictures there remain only some fragments of frescoes which are on exhibit in the Pinacoteca: one of St. Catherine of Siena, and the portrait of Bishop Bartolomeo Vicentini, founder of the Pious Confraternity of the Sacred Crown of Thorns.

The accurate description Friedrich Blume gives of the Ambrosiana Library in the first volume of his *Iter Italicum* published in Berlin in 1824 dates from this time. He came to see it in 1821 and in 1823. His account is also interesting because of the exact list of the days when the library did not open; unfortunately, as in the time of Muratori, the days it was closed (197) considerably outnumbered those when one could get into the library. The catalogues, too, according to Blume, were in deplorable condition. The visit of the Countess Anna Potocka took place in 1826. Three times in three successive years, 1826, 1827 and 1828, a conservator of the libraries of France, Valery, came to study the Ambrosiana manuscripts and then wrote with grateful admiration of the courtesy of the Milanese librarians. Heinrich Heine also visited in 1828.

NOTES

On De Pecis, see the anonymous opusculum (actually written by Bernardo Gatti), *Cenni intorno alla vita ed alle opere di GiuseppePecis*, Milan, 1837. ---On the transformations of the buildings, see L. Gramatica, *L'Ambrosiana: 8 Dicembre 1923*, Milan, Fratelli Treves, 1923. ---A list of holidays and hours open is given by F. Blume, *Iter Italicum*, I, Berlin, 1824, p. 123. ---Valery is the pseudonym of Antoine-Claude Pasquin whose *Voyages historiques et litteraires* were published in Brussells in 1835. ---See the work already cited of Morazzoni, p. l04, for Potocka.

FEDERICO FAGNANI

1775   1840

LASCIO   PER   TESTAMENTO

ALLA   BIBLIOTECA   AMBROSIANA

VENTITREMILA   VOLVMI

QVATTROMILA   TRECENTO   DISEGNI

SEDICIMILA   STAMPE

XI

THE FAGNANI AND CUSTODI DONATIONS

The legacy of the Marchese Federico Fagnani, who died in 1840, was a substantial increment to the library and the Pinacoteca. It included some precious manuscripts, among them a great mass of genealogical information on the noble Lombard families collected by Raffaele Fagnani, 313 15th century editions, 560 volumes edited between 1501 and 1525, seventy editions of *Gerusalemme Liberata*, 22,000 other volumes, most of them rare, as well as 4,200 drawings and 16,025 prints. That posterity might know their gratitude for the generosity of the eminent Milanese bibliophile, the Trustees decided to locate the Fagnani Library in the old "galleria delle statue," available because of recent rebuilding, and to name it after him; to this day it is called the *Sala Fagnani*. A monument raised to him in the middle of the room had to be demolished in 1968 for the construction of the unfortunate new Library tower. The bust, sculpted in 1843 by Giovanni Labus, was relocated on a new marble base in the entrance hall in December 1979.

The donation of Baron Pietro Custodi of Galbiate was resolved upon by a notarized act in 1829, ratified by hand of the royal imperial governor, to go into effect at the baron's death. The assignment to the library took place at the death of the donor on May 14, 1842. The 20,000 Custodi volumes were put in the old "galleria delle pitture," now called the Sala Custodi. The Custodi donation, of which there is a detailed catalogue of assignment, enriched the Ambrosiana with a notable collection chiefly of interest to historians of economics.

On September 11, 1844, under the portico of the Ambrosiana, a grandiose marble statue of Gian Domenico Romagnosi, the renowned work of Abbondio Sangiorgio, was unveiled. The donors were anxious to remove the wooden gate on the door of the library and replace it with one of perforated iron so that the monument could be seen from the street and from the Piazza Mercanti. When the cortile disappeared in 1923, the work of Sangiorgio was enclosed as in a cupboard and no longer visible. It has awaited liberation these sixty years, often promised, still unfulfilled.

Gustave Flaubert went through the rooms of the Ambrosiana in May 1845. At the time he was engaged in the completion of his most noted work, *Madame Bovary*. The novelist found the atmosphere cold and damp and had little to say about the famous manuscripts, contenting himself instead with admiring the Raphael cartoon, remarking on its, "calme et intelligence, verite et force; a gauche, groupe de l'homme qui lit: crane ou l'intelligence transude..."

The library was enriched in 1848 by a gift of six thousand volumes from the lawyer Federico Agnelli. The brothers Jules and Edmond de Goncourt admired the Borgia lock in 1855. The Ambrosiana which, in 1844 had received into its cloister a statue by Romagnosi, widely known to belong to the highest degree of masonry, had no difficulty in 1857 taking on as scribe or custodian of catalogues, a thirty year old priest, Antonio Stoppani, who made no secret of his 'liberal' sympathies, because of which his teaching post at St. Peter Martyr Seminary had been taken from him. The Ambrosiana stipends were not regal at the time, but the thousand Milanese lire a year (equal to 882 Austrian) were a godsend to the young geologist whom the Austrian government tried in every way to boycott. He went on working at the Ambrosiana until 1861 when, with the Austrians gone, it was possible to find better arrangements at the University of Pavia.

It seems that among the solemn celebrations with which the Milanese greeted Vittorio Emanuele II and Napoleon III in June, 1859, was a visit of the two sovereigns to the Ambrosiana.

NOTES

The history of the monument to Romagnosi, now imprisoned in an *ambulacro*, can be found in the interesting article by Filippo Meda, *"L'odissea dei monumenti a G. D. G. Romagnosi,"* in *La Lettura*, Milan, 1-6-1925, p. 451 ff. ---Flaubert, *Voyages*, edited by R. Dumesnil, Paris, 1948, p. 136. ---See A. M. Cornelio, *Vita di Antonio Stoppani*, Milan, 1898, pp. 69-73.

XII

THE TIMES OF CERIANI AND RATTI

On the occasion of the third centenary of the birth of Cardinal Federico (August 18, 1564), the municipal authorities of Milan decided to erect a statue of him in the Piazza San Sepolcro near the old entrance of the library. This was clearly a gesture of reconciliation. The strife between the new Italian government and the Holy See was unhappily serious in those years. The events of '59 created a paradoxical situation in the Milanese Catholic world. A few days after the entry into the city of the Franco-Piedmontese armies, Pius IX appointed Monsignor Paolo Angelo Ballerini Archbishop of Milan despite the fact that he had been proposed to Rome by the Vienna government on the basis of the 1855 concordat between the Holy See and Austria. Faced with the strongest opposition not only of Milanese liberals, but also of the metropolitan Chapter and a significant portion of the clergy (those of the *Societa Ecclesiastica*), Ballerini and his vicar, Caccia, had to go on for years and years sustaining the intransigence of Pius IX which, on a calm appraisal, has to be judged at least imprudent. This conclusive judgment of the Jesuit Father G. Martina can be found in the recent Italian edition of R. Aubert's book on Pius IX.

In 1855, Luigi Biraghi, well known as the worthy founder of the Institute of the Marcelline, was elected Doctor of the Ambrosiana. He had published in 1848 the so-called *Datiana Historia*. As archeologist, he drew down upon himself the ferocious and well-founded criticisms of Mommsen, Morin and Savio. In politics, he nursed sympathies with the liberal current, but out of a desire for peace -- as Castiglioni writes -- "when it was a matter of taking a risk and arguing, he withdrew from the contest."

In that same year of 1855 the twenty seven year old Antonio Maria Ceriani was taken on in the library as keeper of the catalogue. He remained at the Ambrosiana for 52 years: Doctor in 1857, Prefect in 1870. For the history of the following decades it is a curious but noteworthy fact that the first publication of Ceriani appeared on February 11, 1860 in *Il Conciliatore*: it is an extended, accurate and learned review of biblical criticism. *Il Conciliatore* was in 1860 the paper of the Milanese priests belonging to the *Societa Ecclesiastica*, founded to work against any collusion between the religious sovereignty of the Pope and the Austrian influence in Italy. In 1861, Ceriani began the publication of his *Monumenta sacra et profana* and that same year undertook a research trip to England. On January 23, 1862, the thirty-four year old priest was created a Knight of Saints Maurice and Lazarus. This high honor, which took notice of the uncommon civil merit of Ceriani in the field of culture, came from the Italian government, still then in Torino. Against the background of this historic struggle, the initiative of a monument to Cardinal Federico Borromeo must be seen. The Municipality of Milan unveiled it on Sunday, June 16, 1865. Quite naturally, the Doctors and Trustees of the Ambrosiana took part in the ceremony, despite the absence of the diocesan ecclesiastical authority. Giulio Carcano, royal supervisor of studies, in his official discourse, alluded to the unfortunate dissension between Church and State in Italy with these happy words: "Despite the progress made from the 17th Century on, the necessary accord between faith and reason seems still lying hidden in the thoughts of a few timid souls .... I look at this solemn building (the Ambrosiana) that Federico opened and I wonder how others could be induced to follow his generous impulse. For them, there is only this: to love study, continuously to nourish the mind, to encourage knowledge; not to fear it but to go to meet it .... Federigo Borromeo saw in the vast progress of science the victory of religion."

1867 marks the notable gift of Count Giulio Porro Lambertenghi, which brought to the Ambrosiana 47 manuscript codices, 407 incunabula and 142 folders containing the historical memoirs of the Marchese Antonio Botta-Adorno.

Ceriani went a second time to London in 1866 to study the incomparable collection of Syriac codices in the British Museum. In 1874 he saw through the press the Syro-hexaplaris version of Baruch and Jeremiah. In the *Journal des Savants* of 1877, Ernest Renan himself published the highest praises of the young Milanese orientalist's Ambrosiana edition. There is no need to make a list of the scholarly publications of Ceriani, still studied today. The prestige that came to the Ambrosiana because of them was great. It suffices to recall that Wattenback decided to dedicate to the humble Italian priest his *Scripturae Graecae Specimina*, that Steffens honors the name of Ceriani in his *Lateinische Palaeographie*, and that F. Field dedicates the London edition of the fragments of the *hexapla* of Origen to him. The unquestioned high level and quantity of the Prefect's works suffice to explain why those at the Ambrosiana had no time to take part in the ever more ferocious fight between the liberals and the intransigents or temporalists, a struggle that between '70 and '98 reached scandalous intemperance in Milan.

Ceriani was sixty years old when the thirty-one year old Achille Ratti became one of the Doctors of the Ambrosiana, after he had completed his theological studies in Rome and then been assigned to teach various things in the seminary on the Corso Venezia. Having entered the Ambrosiana in November, 1888, he remained a member of the library for twenty-six years. Trained for twenty years in the school of Ceriani, sharing both work and life, the future pope acquired a passion for learned research, rigorous method, and the conviction that patient study of old texts helps to make a turbid atmosphere serene and prepares for better days. Others have said much of the scholarly labors of Achille Ratti. The best of them deal with the history of the Church of Milan; they remain worthwhile contributions. He had the basic talent necessary for writing history, an extremely lucid intelligence. Cesare Cantu says that Manzoni "agrees with Thiers that the mark of the historian comes down to understanding; color, morality, erudition and philosophy mean nothing if the facts are not understood."

Ratti also had the courage of the truth, that is, of saying the truth even when it did not please or could cause harm. His priestly cloth notwithstanding, despite the impoverished culture of the great part of his colleagues, despite the wind that still blew in high places, already in the year 1897 Ratti supported and publicized the conclusions of Duchesne concerning the pretended apostolic origins of the church of Milan; he wrote clearly and unmistakably that the tradition of St. Barnabas was a legend without foundation. This Doctor of the Ambrosiana did not fear to correct even Pastor. Cardinal Matthew Schiner might have been beyond reproach after becoming a cardinal, but a document in the Archives of Milan showed that a certain Giovanni Schiner, designated heir of half the cardinal's goods, "was, alas, a youthful sin of the future prince of the Church." Ratti made public this discovery at the fourth international scientific congress of Catholics held in August, 1897 in Fribourg, Switzerland. Antonio Ceruti, his colleague as Doctor, had made a copy of the metropolitan codex of Goffredo da Bussero. Ratti, in a monograph of 1901, praised the diligence of his colleague but knew his work was a bit simplistic and he did not hesitate to write in the *Archivio Storico Lombardo* that the copy of the codex made by Ceruti was "to be used with much caution." In the same monograph, he speaks of that "great man" L. A. Muratori, but provides evidence of "two quite Homeric nods" of the famous historian who was his predecessor. Ratti had the courage to consign to the pulping machine his colleague Giovanni Crivelli's collection of the youthful letters of St. Charles, of which 38 quires (608 pages) were already printed, because the edition did not meet the demands of serious criticism.

Giuseppe Fumagalli, who was a fellow librarian, has written of Ratti the librarian in a little book published by Formiggini in 1925. Fumagalli was in retirement in 1921, but from 1899 to 1912 he was director of the Braidense Library and could thus remember from close up when he wrote that Ratti "had to a high degree those virtues peculiar to the profession and which of themselves suffice to make a good librarian; they make an excellent one when, as in his case, they combine with a versatile culture: order, minute exactitude, the greatest love for books ... But Ratti the librarian had another virtue which not all his colleagues can claim: exquisite courtesy of manners, supreme patience with visitors and even with indiscreet scholars. One who had recourse to him (and here Fumagalli alludes to his own relations with Ratti) never did so in vain and will not forget how easily assistance, complete, urbane, solid, was had."

Fumagalli also summarizes what Ratti did for the Pinacoteca: "even before assuming the prefecture of the Library (in 1907), he had accomplished the reordering of that glorious institute which is his greatest accomplishment. The new arrangement given to the Ambrosiana and especially to the artistic collections of pictures, drawings, engravings, is exclusively due to him and to the tenacity with which he was able to overcome the not inconsiderable technical and financial difficulties as well as the resistance of the good Ceriani, still alive when this work of transformation was begun and completed. Averse by character and age to all innovation, Ceriani had such trust in and love for Ratti that he gave him a free hand. The re-ordering was completed in the years 1905 and 1906, with the work of Luigi Cavenaghi, Luca Beltrami and Antonio Grandi; not only through Ratti's initiative but also by his personal effort, the scattered collections of the Settala Museum, the oldest museum of Milan, one of the oldest and most important in Italy, was then restored to its original condition ...." The Settala Museum was restored by bringing together everything that could be found and putting it in one place on the ground floor, on the left as you enter. Then the most important prints and the most beautiful drawings were permanently placed in special glass cabinets chosen according to a standard which today seems ruinous.

The many works promoted by Ratti involved heavy expenses and by 1907 the pot was nearly empty. Prefect Ratti considered seeking a subsidy from the central administrative commission of grants of the Cassa di Risparmio delle Provincie Lombarde. "I wanted to see the land before landing," he himself wrote in recounting the episode. "In principle, my request of subsidy was approved, but some rigid interpreters of the statute held that the Library could not be included among beneficiaries properly speaking. There then came to my mind a wonderful page of Cardinal Federico's in which he exhorted those without children and near relatives to remember this work in their wills, 'the usefulness of which will be perpetual and a great glory to God, something valuable not only to Italy but to other nations as well,' and thought that the central commission answered to the conditions he had laid down. That was enough. And I remembered that Manzoni, in *I Promessi Sposi*, in reference to the one hundred thousand scudi invested by Borromeo in the library, wrote among other things: 'There are perhaps still some who think that grants of this sort, indeed all grants, are the best and most useful alms.' Very well, Cardinal Federico and Manzoni were as one in thinking that subsidies to the Ambrosiana count as true benefices, indeed the best! So I did not hesitate. I copied the two passages and sent them to all the members of the central commission of benefices. These worthy gentlemen were unanimous, and after them the authorities, in accepting the views of the two great Milanese."

By a *motu proprio* of Vittorio Emanuele III of September 30, 1906, Achille Ratti was named a Knight of the Order of Saints Maurice and Lazarus because -- so read the citation -- " he merits it for his historical studies and has brought to completion the rearrangement of the Ambrosiana Library and Gallery." The act cited other patriotic contributions of Ratti as well. We mentioned above the "liberal" leanings of Biraghi and Ceriani, that is, their sympathy with the new Italian state. The patriotism of the men of the Ambrosiana was underscored during the decades Ratti spent at the Ambrosiana, all the more so because Ratti had a better opportunity than most to feel first hand the evil fruit of some of the deplorable press campaigns of the priest-journalist Davide Albertario. Underlying the repeated visits of Queen Margherita of Savoy to the Ambrosiana were motives other than cultural ones. Achille Ratti's patriotism found various ways and opportunities to express itself. Worth recalling is the following. In 1896, the *Circolo Filologico Milanese* promoted a series of lectures on the history of the city. The topic "The Ambrosian Church" was assigned to Ratti, and his lecture chanced to be scheduled during the days of the Adua disaster. In the book published by the Bocca Brothers in 1897, which contains these "Lectures on Milanese History," Ratti added to his: "Only a summary of this lecture could be given to the audience because of the unspeakable suffering which in those days afflicted every Italian heart. It is put before the reader after a distant but certain voice has announced that there can be hope of a new prospect (for the liberation of the Italian prisoners) something for which so many mothers have sighed, firmly trusting in the outlook and demeanor of the one who, calling an old pontiff the Father of all, now renounces being the enemy of those who are neighbours and sons of that Father. May the promise be fulfilled." Ratti alludes to the intervention of Leo XIII in the liberation of the Italian soldiers who remained prisoners at Adua and were interned in the Scioa. Filippo Meda reprinted this postscript in 1932, pointing out the ponderous diplomatic caution with which Ratti expressed his patriotic and religious feelings: "here already was the man Pius XI would later be."

These precedents partly explain why the Ambrosiana was considered neutral territory during the sad days of May, 1898, and why Ratti could act as official mediator between Archbishop Ferrari and General Bava Beccaris. For the history of the Milan "riots" of May 1898 as well as for the history of the Ambrosiana, the four letters Ratti wrote just at that time to his friend, the Belgian Jesuit Francis Van Ortroy, then in Rome, seem to me of great historical importance. Since they have never been published, I include them in the notes to this chapter as something flattering to many Milanese. Ratti wrote these letters with great care and clearly not only for his Jesuit friend; he wished to inform through his friend those editing *La Civilta Cattolica* and perhaps others higher up as to what the situation in Milan really was, polemics in the press apart.

Considering his personal experience in '98, it can be better understood why Achille Ratti, when he became pope in 1922, immediately wished to arrive at a conciliation of the Holy See with the Italian government at all costs.

Noteworthy acquisitions, donations and additions came about in those years. The magnificent Piumati edition of the *Codice Atlantico* was published between 1894 and 1904 "with a subsidy from the King and Government." Monsignor Carlo Nardi's gift of some five thousand volumes was made in 1903, and another library came as a gift from Duke Tommaso Gallarati Scotti. The Trotti collection amounting to some 460 manuscripts (from the 10th to the 18th centuries) came to the Ambrosiana in 1907, the munificent gift of the Marchesa Maria Trotti Belgiojoso and the Marchese Ludovico Trotti Bentivoglio; originally it formed part of the Trivulziana Library. In 1909 Donna Rachele Villa Pernice donated autographs and the private archive of Cesare Beccaria to the Ambrosiana also enriching the Ambrosiana with twenty thousand volumes of the Villa Pernice library.

In November, 1909, Ratti promoted a subscription in Milan so as to acquire the 1610 Arabic codices that the magentine businessman Giuseppe Caprotti had collected during thirty-four years of residence in Yemen and wished to sell. Within a week Ratti had found twenty-five Milan benefactors who offered the thirty thousand 1909 lire needed. Senator Luca Beltrami made numerous gifts of letters, drawings and objects of art during the Ratti years. In 1911 Duke Tommaso Gallarati Scotti, grandfather of the author of the *Vita di Antonio Fogazzaro*, made a gift to the Ambrosiana of the famous manuscript of Gellius illustrated by Guglielmo Giraldi in 1448.

On November 13, 1913, Prefect Ratti informed the Royal Lombard Institute of three new donations: a thousand volumes of history and biblical science of the astronomer Giovanni Schiaparelli; the collections of Enrico Osnago: 200 volumes on numismatics, about 800 of Napoleonic history; 4000 coins, 900 of them Milanese; the De Vries collection of codices reproduced in thirty volumes of large format, a gift of the noble Doctor Giuseppe Marietti, who had already given to the Ambrosiana the entire Teubner collection of Latin and Greek classics.

In March 1907, Ceriani died and Achille Ratti became Prefect in name as for some years already he had been in fact. At this time of agitated religious discussion a biblicist joined the Ambrosiana. Ratti, reaffirming the more than Milanese character of the Ambrosiana, as laid down in the constitution of Cardinal Federico, brought to Milan in August 1909 a young priest from Brescia, Luigi Gramatica, and had him elected a Doctor. In 1892-1893, Gramatica had spent two years in Palestine studying the Bible in biblical settings at the school of Father Lagrange; he knew both Hebrew and Arabic and in 1909 was preparing a new edition of the *Clementine Vulgate*. This appeared in 1923, printed by Cappelli at Rocca San Casciano. Gramatica contributed to it not only his prolonged labor but much of his own and his two sisters' money as well. There was a second printing in 1914 published by Hoepli, Benziger and Gil of Barcelona. It was acquired by the most important universities and libraries throughout the world, received high praise even from non-Catholic scholars and brought notable prestige to Cardinal Federico's institution. In November 1911, Pope Pius X named Achille Ratti Vice Prefect of the Vatican Library; he made the move to Rome at the end of 1913. On September 26, 1914, Ratti as a retired Doctor succeeded in having Gramatica elected prefect.

NOTES

G. Martina's judgment is in R. Aubert, *Il Pontificato di Pio IX*, Turin, 1964, p. 808. ---On Biraghi, see C. Castiglioni, *Calabiana e i suoi tempi*, Milan, 1942, p. 179. ---Giulio Carcano's discourse in *Opere Complete*, Vol. V, Milan, 1894, p. 380. ---Notification of Porro Lambertenghi's donation is in *Arch. St. Lomb.*, 1886, II, p. 732. ---On Ceriani, see F. Parente, *Dizionario Biografico degli Italiani*, 23, 1979, pp. 737-43. ---On Manzoni's conception of the historian, see *Opere*,Vol. III, Milan, 1950, p. 633. ---Ratti's courage with respect to the truth is discussed by Paolo Bellezza in his introduction to Ratti (Pius XI), *Scritti Storici*, Florence, 1932, p. XVII. ---Ratti's criticisms of Ceruti and Muratori in *Arch. St. Lomb.*, 1901, I, pp. 10 and 16. ---The remarks of Giuseppe Fumagalli are contained in the wonderful little book entitled *Achille Ratti*, published by Formiggini in 1925. ---Ratti's request of the *Cassa di Risparmio* of 1907 (not 1911!) is also recorded by Bellezza in the introduction mentioned, p. XXXI and by G. Galbiati, *Papa Pio XI*, Milan, 1939, pp. 30-32. Dr. Nino Gutierrez speaks of it in *Storia di Milano, Fond. Treccani*, XV, Milan. 1962, pp. 971-2. As a result of Ratti's request 4,000 Lire were given the

Ambrosiana in 1907, 30,000 in 1908, 20,000 in 1910 and 14,000 in 1914. ---F. Meda republished the gloss in the journal *L'Italia*, April 2, 1932. We give below the four letters written by Achille Ratti to Fr. van Ortroy in 1898:

I

(The first, dated May 8, 1898, begins by telling his friend of the appointment of Giovanni Mercati as *scrittore* in the Vatican Library.)

... we have suffered a heavy loss, doubly difficult and painful for me who not only admire the teaching and industry but also appreciate the outstanding gifts of spirit of Mercati and have profited from the friendship that binds me to him. But so it is --what's done is done -- and so it will be.

I cannot say these words without thinking of all that is happening around me. We are passing through sad days: yesterday a real revolution, bloody and pugnacious, in many parts of the city. The Ambrosiana was not disturbed but in the Via Torino and in the Via Armorari and at the mouths of the Via Asole and Valpetrosa were many dead and wounded. Today a state of siege has been proclaimed and the city is under military occupation; even as I write (about one in the afternoon) the sound of firearms is audible. There were more serious disturbances at the Porta Nuova but so far as I know the residence of the Jesuit Fathers was not disturbed. At the Cenacle too everything is tranquil. The poor Canossians of S. Michele alla Chiusa, on the other hand, were seriously threatened. Food was a problem here as in many other places; clearly we are being put to the first serious test by the socialists and anarchists. It is even clearer that the authorities were caught by surprise. We hope, if indeed it is hopeable, that the experience will teach a few things .... The Duchess Scotti hopes you have received her answer; she and her whole household greet you. Everything is going well, Tommasino happy because of a short visit to Florence for the First Communion of his cousin Zaccaria. The disorders of recent days have caused apprehension there, particularly after the vandalism at the house of the Marchese Saporiti (who luckily was with the Marchesa absent from Milan), but the charity and almsgiving of the two good oldsters will always be a secure defense of the Scotti house. And how go things in Rome?

II

Milan, May 21, 1898

Reverend Father and Dearest Friend,

I owe you so much and I myself am confused. Believe me, it is not my fault: for fifteen days I have had no arms, no head, no time, I have been so harassed by and absorbed in the grave public need. My relations, of which you have some knowledge, the neutral position of the Ambrosiana and a complex of momentous circumstances have placed a serious responsibility on me that I could not have refused without seeming a man without a head, heart or conscience. You can see it is not a pretty situation.   I would like to explain everything to you in person so I firmly hope and profoundly desire that when you return to the fatherland you will spend at least several days in Milan; otherwise it will be you who is at fault. Calm and security have returned here, though not for the Cardinal Archbishop. The accusations of complicity launched against him and the Catholics are absurd and everyone begins to grasp this; so too the taint of meanness of soul and fear of which he is accused. It is nonetheless true that circumstances were peculiarly against him and that he was served and advised in the worst possible way and by those who owed him the most. His flank was exposed and he was beaten in the breach and all the hatred, resentment and personalities (sic) accumulated in the course of four years were unleashed at one time; this most unlucky time became a steel comb which found all the snarls, and there were indeed many though they were multiplied and exaggerated in an artful way. It is hard to imagine how his position here has suffered; I still do not know if it can be redeemed. Today, and only today, I hope that his position can be bettered a little after much effort with General Bava who is often in the most influential circles. C. Ottavio Cornaggia is of great help to me, the *Lega Lombarda* has done all it can and has conducted itself splendidly. Those who think otherwise do not take into account the exceptional difficulties created by the circumstances, by the person of the Archbishop, by the state of siege, by public opinion, the press, the parties. All depends now on the attitude taken by the Holy See. I have written to Monsignor Angeli (let this be between us) offering to provide information, knowing that he is very badly informed. The Capuchins were not imprisoned but treated with special regard; the *Civilta* (which wants to take an interest in our affairs) would do well to take this into account as a result of what the *Lega* published. *L'Osservatore Romano* would do well to correct its position and not insist on the suppression of the Diocesan Committee of unhappy memory, a suppression which because of the circumstances has lost practically all its value, especially since the government now seems disposed to permit its reconstitution (let this be between us). It is important that *L'Osservatore Romano* break its silence regarding the Cardinal just to show that the Holy See not abandon him to his fate, at least not without coming calmly and soberly to his defense: circumstances could not possibly seem or be more adverse for him. All the more should account be taken of the intemperate ways he has been treated, particularly by the press in the first days without regard for the principle and whole order of ideas and things he represents. It could render a real service by making known these things and recommending the greatest caution and attention in dealing with our local facts; it is the *Lega* that can provide them to you and exactly. The *Unita Cattolica* only makes things worse and would do well to be silent. You would do me a great favor by informing me accurately on the ideas and bearing of Cardinal Parocchi. What does he think of the political elections? What does he say about our Cardinal? ---What do those who have a voice in the Capitol tell you of these things? Especially Cardinal Rampolla? Difficult questions, but you will understand me well enough and will know how to find answers. (....)

So many things for Father Ehrle. Paul Sabatier wrote me; I will answer him tomorrow. Now I can go to bed, it is already one in the morning and I must be up at six. Pray for me and be assured that I am affectionaly yours.
A. Ratti.

III
Milan, June 3, 1898

My dear Father,

I begin to wonder if you received my last letter. I should be disappointed, not so much for all the questions I put to you because of the present state of things and the judgments I made on them, but for all the thanks ....

The grievously serious recent events have had their impact here as well, even more than elsewhere, though the suppressions and dissolutions have been conducted less severely here than, for example, at Bergamo and Reggio. The Pontifical letter was a heavy blow to our Cardinal Archbishop, whose position here remains most precarious. Do you know the reaction to it, especially by those promoting the electionist movement among Catholics? Whatever you can tell me on this matter will be of great help.

I will stop here because I am extremely short of time. Wish me well and be assured that I am your most affectionate friend

S. A. Ratti

P.S. Is it true that Father Zocchi spoke against Monsignor Bonomelli? Mercati, Fumagalli, Ambrosoli, have been elected corresponding members of the Institute.

IV

Milan, June 14, 1898

Dearest Father,

I thank you very much for the letter you found time to write in the midst of all your labors. Only one thing in it surprised me and that was the connection made between the pontifical letter and my letter to Monsignor Angeli. I wrote two letters to him; the second (footnote: May 24) which might have provided some light arrived in Rome when the *Osservatore Romano* and the *Voce della Verita* had already published the pontifical document; the first only endorsed the call for help of our Cardinal Archbishop whose position was made more difficult by the silence of the *Osservatore Romano*. But when you are here we can more easily discuss this and other things. We are now awaiting the trial of Albertario and company. *La Lega Lombarda* has published the indictment (and was confiscated because of it, but only 12 copies of an all but exhausted edition and without further consequences) which does not make it easy to predict the outcome. Whatever the result, I think it will go from bad to worse for our poor Cardinal, all the more so if the flood of lies does not stop, but it seems rather to increase ....
But enough on that for now. Best wishes from our friends, to all of whom I have given your regards and all of whom wish to be remembered to you. Believe me your most affectionate friend.

S. A. Ratti

(These and other letters of A. Ratti are preserved in the library of the Bollandists (24 Boulevard Saint-Michel, Bruxelles). I must thank Fathers M. Coens, B. de Gaiffier and F. Halkin for receiving me in their library in the summer of 1965.)

XIII

THE REBUILDING OF 1921-1923

Many acquisitions had made urgent the need of breathing space for both the Library and the Gallery. The directors of the institute, that is, the prefect Luigi Gramatica, and the trustee Marco Magistretti, invited the most prominent citizens of Milan to a reunion on May 17, 1921: the doctor Silvio Crespi, the lawyer Filippo Meda, the engineer Cesare Saldini, the engineer Angelo Salmoiraghi, and many others. They all viewed with approval Gramatica's plan to transform the Cortile of Moraglia into a new reading room. The project was entrusted to the architect Ambrogio Annoni. The ordinary administration of the Ambrosiana, always short of means, could not handle the cost of so important a work. A "Pro Ambrosiana" committee was formed with the lawyer Filippo Meda as president and the engineer Cesare Saldini as vice-president. They were soon joined by a Committee of the Women of Milan.

It should be remembered that in 1918 the former prefect, Achille Ratti, had been sent to Poland as representative of the Holy See and remained there 37 months. Then, on June 13, 1921, he was chosen Archbishop of Milan and created cardinal. On September 8 of that same year he made his solemn entrance into Milan and the following day paid an official visit on the

Ambrosiana. After little more than four months of residence in Milan he became head of the Church on February 6, 1922, as Pope Pius XI. It was the first time in history that a librarian had become pope; he had lived "hidden among books" until his sixtieth year. The Ambrosiana enjoyed an enormous amount of reflected publicity.

Nor was it difficult to find many generous supporters from among the *Amici dell'Ambrosiana* which had been organized even before Cardinal Ratti came to Milan. The most famous benefactors of the building improvements of 1921-1923 were Pope Pius XI (fifty thousand lire); the heirs of Giuseppe Marietti, that is the Nobles Dr. Luigi, the engineer Carlo and Giannino Radice Fossati (fifty thousand lire); the *Cassa di Risparmio delle Provincie Lombarde.* (forty thousand lire); the Trustees of the Ambrosiana (fifty thousand lire). The humble too contributed to the initiative: a Miss Luisa Gritti managed to collect sixty thousand 1922 lire. Many others helped and their names are engraved in marble at the entrance.

In those same years the noble family Gallarati Scotti gave some valuable paintings: the St. Ambrose of Figino, the triptych of Vivarini. The Marietti heirs enriched the picture gallery with another Bruegel. The l921-1923 construction meant a substantial expansion of the Federician complex. The new reading room had a ceiling of reinforced concrete, sustained by four crossbeams with a metal framework to support the glass ceiling. The subsoil of the area, which before had been a courtyard and collected rainwater, was drained; it was then restored with a wasps nest maze of tunnels providing both ventilation and winter heat. The resulting new room was a square, 15 meters a side, with an area of 1900 cubic meters, capable of accomodating a hundred readers and about four thousand reference works on the open shelves. The shelves on the outer walls hold another eight thousand volumes. It remains today among the most beautiful reading rooms in Milan. The opening took place December 8, 1923, with Cardinal G. Bisleti representing the Holy See, Professor Gioacchino Volpe representing the government, and other officials of Milan.

Luigi Gramatica resigned in September 1924 when he was called to Rome by his old colleague Pius XI. "The Missionary Exposition," wrote *L'Osservatore Romano* in 1935, "should be covered by a periodical publication whose director ought to be a man of vast erudition in the fields of Church history and geography. No one could come to the task better prepared than Monsignor Gramatica, who edits with exceptional skill the

Rivista Illustrata dell'Esposizione Missionaria." No one in Milan could believe this official version. Everyone thought that his resignation was the result of an incident the previous year. On February 12, 1923, Gramatica gave a talk at the *Universita Cattolica*'s celebration of the first anniversary of the coronation of Pius XI. Cardinals Tosi and Laurenti were present. Gramatica candidly asserted that "nothing in the scholarly, priestly or simply human background of Ratti would have led one to expect his elevation to the Supreme Chair." Speaking after the official orator, Cardinal Laurenti begged to differ with Gramatica's assertion. This is the source of the legend that Gramatica's resignation as Prefect of the library stemmed from his infelicitous words. The fine pages devoted to Gramatica by the *Bollettino Parrocchiale di Rovato* in April, 1950 should be consulted. The true story is something else. In November 1921, Monsignor Marco Magistretti, president of the Trustees, the friend of Gramatica and wholehearted supporter of the building improvements undertaken by him, died. The next president, Giuseppe Confalonieri, belonged to the group of people who already at the end of 1912 regarded Gramatica as an "intruder" in the Ambrosiana. The disagreement between the two became unbridgeable. The abusive and unwarranted intrusions of Confalonieri became open criticism of the work in progress. As has been said, the new reading room was inaugurated on December 8, 1923 with Cardinal Gaetano Bisleti, Prefect of the Congregation of Seminaries and of Universities, in attendance. The preceding November, Gramatica sent a memo to Bisleti, followed by other letters, and laid out clearly Confalonieri's intrigues against him as well as the miserable personnel at his disposal and the starvation wages they received.

Confalonieri too sent Bisleti a memo in the name of the Trustees with a list of Gramatica's alleged wrongs together with the request that he be given "some other post, on a board or a professorship." The major complaint was that Gramatica held that "the Federician constitution was no longer in force because it did not fit the times and had fallen partly in desuetude." Giovanni Mercati, then a *scrittore* in the Vatican Library, followed with emotion the tribulations of his friend Gramatica and in June 1924 offered him a good and honorable position in Rome. Gramatica, although he felt that his resignation, after he had borne such burdens in the building of the new reading room, amounted to unjust humiliation, accepted Mercati's proposal and his assurance of every support from the highest echelons of Roman authority. With Gramatica gone, Giovanni Galbiati, who had become known because of a fine book on the sources of

Cicero's *De Republica*, was elected Prefect in October, 1924 by the all but explicit designation of Pius XI.

NOTES

Interesting particulars on Gramatica's succession to Ratti are found in N. Vian, *"Una illustre successione alla Biblioteca Vaticana: Achille Ratti,"* in *Melanges Eugene Tisserant*, VII, Citta del Vaticano, 1964, pp. 373-439. --The Italian and foreign benefactors are all accurately listed in the opusculum of L. Gramatica already cited: *L'Ambrosiana, 8 Dicembre 1923.* ---Something on the resignation of Gramatica in 1924 can be found in the *Bollettino Parocchiale of Rovato, 1950: the legend of the "unhappy phrase" is told here as true. Both Gramatica's and Confalonieri's memos are preserved in the archives of the Sacred Congregation for Catholic Education. The niece of Monsignor Gramatica, Professor Carolina Zilani, in 1967-68 donated to the Ambrosiana many letters and other correspondence of her uncle.*

XIV

THE GIFT OF PIUS XI

In 1926 the Ambrosiana received the Arab library of Eugenio Griffini Bey comprising 56 manuscripts as well as 1200 printed works. A catalogue of this library was published by Dr. Angela Codazzi. This book includes as well a complete biography of Griffini, written by his cousin Luca Beltrami, plus the story of the sixty cases of Yemenic manuscripts collected by Caprotti, entrusted to the custody of Griffini and eventually acquired by Prefect Ratti in 1909. From 1920 to 1925 Griffini was conservator in Cairo of the library of King Fuad of Egypt.

Pope Ratti retained a most lively interest in his Ambrosiana. At his wish the Benedictine Germain Morin came here to begin the cataloguing of the Bobbio codices in 1925-1926. As he had in other libraries, the French monk found unedited Augustinian works in the Ambrosiana. But working conditions were truly bad and for that reason, and because of certain misunderstandings with Prefect Galbiati, he sought and found in July 1926 a better situation in Bavaria at Munich.

A bronze of Pius XI was unveiled in the reading room on March 20, 1927. In his turn, the pope was preparing for "his Ambrosiana" a truly regal gift. By abolishing the parish of San Sepolcro and transferring elsewhere the motherhouse of the

Oblates, the library and gallery could be substantially expanded. The greater part of the houses around the old church of the Crusaders was transformed into offices making it, like so many other city parishes, empty of people. The Motherhouse of the Oblate Fathers was a greater obstacle; in 1581 St. Charles had given the church of San Sepolcro to the congregation of Oblates founded by himself, attaching to it various contiguous houses for their common life. The saint himself used to come to San Sepolcro nearly every week to pray and preach. For centuries the house of San Sepolcro had been the heart of the Congregation of Oblates. But Pius XI, having lived twenty-six years in the Ambrosiana, knew how religiously effective an institute of culture can be. And a pope could say authoritatively that the sacrifice asked of the Oblates was not too heavy considering the great good that would accrue to the institution of Cardinal Federico. A decree of Archbishop Tosi of July 6, 1928 suppressed the parish of San Sepolcro; another royal decree of November 29 gave civil effect to the decision of the archbishop. The last Oblates living next to church moved on March 1919 to a house on the Corso Magenta.

It was thus possible for Prefect Giovanni Galbiati to undertake a totally new disposition of the gallery, readapting the space, transforming into galleries the crumbling old place previously inhabited by the Oblates. The Settala museum was transferred to the second floor, to one of the little rooms around the cortile of marbles. Imposing and grandiose work was done for which Galbiati made use of the services of the architects Ambrogio Annoni and Alessandro Minali. The new work was completed May 25, 1932 and inaugurated as the conclusion of the celebration of the third centenary of the death of Cardinal Federico (September 21, 1631).

At this time G. Morazzoni published the monograph *L'Ambrosiana nel terzo centenario di Federico Borromeo*, Milan, 1932. Six plates in this book reproduce works of art given to the Ambrosiana by the Counts Cattaneo di Proh; it should be noted that these works of art remained for only a brief season in the Ambrosiana since, for curious reasons, they had to be returned to the incautious donor.

In 1926 donna Carlotta Casanova gave to the Ambrosiana the library of her departed husband, the nobleman Enrico (1865-1903); it included manuscripts containing research into the noble families of Lombardy and a notable number of rare and precious books.

The correspondence that Bishop Geremia Bonomelli had left on his death to his faithful friend and secretary Monsignor Emilio Lombardi was an important acquisition. It contained more than fifteen thousand letters that the famous bishop of Cremona received from 1872 to 1914. Some letters of particular importance are in special folders, for example those from Queen Margherita, those from St. Pius X, the letters of his polemics with *L'Osservatore Romano.*

Monsignor Guido Astori, executing the will of Monsignor Lombardi, turned the Bonomelli letters over to the Ambrosiana in 1927. The library of Professor Carlo Salvioni (†$1920), the gift of his widow, Enrichetta, came to the Ambrosiana in 1929: more than 12 thousand printed works and about 30 thousand manuscript sheets. Salvioni was from Bellinzona but he always lived in Italy and he gave Italy two sons in their twenties, called to the front in May, 1916. It was also in 1929 that the collection *Fontes Ambrosiani,* an unquestionable achievement of Prefect Giovanni Galbiati was begun. For the twenty-seven volumes of the *Fontes Ambrosiani* he published, Galbiati himself had to find *"i mezzi di fortuna,"* since the administration of the library could give him no help.

When Donna Rachele Cantu widow of Angelo Villa Pernice died in 1919 she left in trust with the knight and engineer Giulio Martelli of Milan the correspondence of her father Cesare Cantu, comprising fifty years of correspondence with the leading literary and politcal figures of the late 19th Century. In 1932 Giulio Martelli made a gift of the Cantu correspondence to the Ambrosiana.

On October 26, 1932, in order to meet with the archbishop, Cardinal Schuster, the head of state, Benito Mussolini, came to the Ambrosiana.

The villa of the sculptor Lodovico Pogliaghi at Sacro Monte in Varese with all the various collections of art that it contained was annexed in 1937 to the Ambrosiana. The vicissitudes connected with this donation are fully told by Giovanni Galbiati in the volume published in 1959 in honor of Pogliaghi (N. XXXIII of the *Fontes Ambrosiani*). It was on the occasion of the legal proceedings connected with the Pogliaghi bequest that Pius XI wrote the chirograph dated April 27, 1937, published with comments in *La Scuola Cattolica* in June, 1939 by Filippo Meda. In this document the pontiff reaffirms the permanent value of the bull of Paul V (1608) that is, that "the Ambrosiana has its own personality, free from all subordination to other authority not intended by the founder himself, but directly to the Holy See, being thus guaranteed perpetual autonomy both with respect to its patrimony and its government."

On June 23, 1939, due to the liberality of the musical *maestro* Leone Sinigaglia and of his sister Alina Segre Sinigaglia, to honor the memory of their father Abramo Alberto Sinigaglia, the Ambrosiana Library came into possession of a collection of miniatures, glass, bronzes and some ancient Italian Majolica ware. The most important nucleus is represented by a collection of minuscule portraits painted on horn or ivory, many of which are of exquisite craftsmanship. A catalogue of them has been published by Giuseppe Morazzoni. The Sinigaglia collection is now on exhibition in the Sala di Raffaello.

NOTES

The story of the house and church of San Sepolcro can be found in G. Galbiati, *Il tempio dei Crociati e degli Oblati*, Milan, 1930. ---For Casanova's letters, see E. Casanova, *Nobilta Lombarda, Genealogie*, edited by G. Bascape, Milan, 1930.---On the Bonomelli letters, cf. the article of G. Astori in *Vita e Pensiero*, 1931, pp. 640-644.

XV

THE RUINS OF 1943

At the beginning of the Second World War there was the extremely difficult problem of transporting to safe places sheltered from possible war damage the huge and voluminous collections of the Ambrosiana. The most important pictures from the gallery and the most precious manuscripts from the libraries found generous asylum in the steel plated vaults of the *Cassa di Risparmio delle Provincie Lombarde.* Into the subterranean area of the Duomo were taken the many manuscripts and minutes of St. Charles and of Cardinal Federico as well as the collections of the incunabula. Most of the other manuscripts were transported to the Abbazia di Pontida. To the seminary of Arona were sent the hundreds of paintings of lesser importance. Provisions should have been made for the mass of printed books as well. Unfortunately, either by unpardonable imprudence or because of lack of means, the printed books remained on their old shelves. Some damage was caused by the raid of February 14, 1943. Six months later disaster struck. On the night between the 15th and 16th of August the Ambrosiana too was hit heavily and the greater part of the old Federician construction was destroyed or damaged. Through the roof of the old reading room fell, not bombs, but many incendiary sticks, and all the 17th century

wooden cabinets and shelving, full of books, fell prey to the flames. The ceilings of the old Borromeo room and of the Sala Luini also crumbled; the fresco of the Coronation was saved because the Superintendent of the galleries had had the foresight to raise a close fitting protective wall. The flames that night, because of the lack of water in the adjacent streets and the impossiblity of help, there being people to save in all parts of the city, were able to rage for hours and hours and to reach even the Settala museum and destroy most of the furnishings and objects on display. Only the bare walls remained. The losses of printed volumes in the Sala Antica, which contained practically all the 16th century editions bought by the founder and many 17th century books, were severe. The Bazzero armory which stood in the Sala Luini was destroyed. Also destroyed was the whole Japanese collection donated by Carlo Giussani in 1908 which had been located in the Sala Borromeo. The collection of opera librettos of La Scala, which had been in little rooms around the marble courtyard, was destroyed; it contained all the copies that had been given to the censor prior to performances. No need to say, of course, that elsewhere, in Milan, as at the Trivulziana Library and the State Archives, many thousands of manuscript letters and documents also burned whereas the Ambrosiana manuscripts were dispersed and thus saved. But that is meager comfort when one thinks of the pricelessness of the library's patrimony which was irremediably lost and which could have been and should have been saved.

NOTES

On the heavy damage suffered by the libraries and archives of Milan in 1943, see E. Apolloni, *La ricostruzione delle biblioteche italiane dopo la guerra 1940-45*, Direzione Generale delle Accademie e Biblioteche, Ministro della Pubblica Instruzione, Roma, 1949. It is impossible to understand why the directors of the Amrbosiana in 1946-49 did not communicate to the Director General the loss to the Ambrosiana, which seems to have been on the order of eighty thousand volumes, as well as the damage to the premises.

XVI

THE LABORIOUS RECONCONSTRUCTION

It would have been idle to hope that the public authorities would have had the time or the means during the months immediately following the end of hostilities to provide for dispersed libraries and temporarily closed museums. The necessities of daily life were simply more urgent.

To find some immediate aid, the administration of the Ambrosiana planned an exhibition in neighboring Switzerland of the masterworks of art and of the most beautiful and precious manuscripts. Thus the exhibition entitled *Italienische Kunst* was held in Lucerne from July 6 to October 31, 1946.

The idea received the generous agreement of the Swiss and Italian authorities.

There were crowds of visitors.

The Holy See too favored the exhibition: through the good offices of the Secretary of State, Monsignor Giovanni Battista Montini, Pope Pius XII in an act of exceptional courtesy consented to the showing of the San Gerolamo. The famous painting by Leonardo was transported to Lucerne on June 13, 1946. With manuscripts, books and pictures back in place, though many with as yet unrepaired damage, the Ambrosiana reopened its doors to the public with a solemn ceremony on June 13, 1948.

The Ambrosiana took part by means of the majority of its primitive etchings in the exposition of Lombard art treasuries organized by Fernanda Wittgens in Zurich from November 1948 to March 1949. Subsequently it participated in the exposition of treasuries of Italian libraries held in the summer of 1950 at the *Bibliotheque Nationale* in Paris, sending its most famous pictures. An important acquisition for the Ambrosiana came about in 1949 when the library of Count Giacomo Mellorio (†1847) was brought to Milan from the Certosa of Pavia. He had left his library to the monks of Certosa with the proviso that it should go to the Ambrosiana if the monks were ever expelled from Certosa. That in fact took place in 1866. In general the more than eight thousand volumes of the Mellerio donation are elegant and expensive editions.

Long and difficult negotiations, conducted in Rome by the Trustees, were brought to a successful issue in 1951-52 when the Ministeries of Public Works and of Public Instruction recognized the right of the Ambrosiana to compensation for war damages. At that time began the work of restoring the destroyed areas under the aegis of the Minstry of Public Works. The Ministry of Public Instruction, through the Bibliographical Superintendent of Lombardy, spent more than 36 million to have constructed by Lips Vago the new nine storey library tower, to provide with new metal bookshelves the Sale Borromeo, Federiciana, Iemale and Custodi as well as new lighting, and to install a safe and new *refrattari corazzati* in the Sala Prefeto. The new library tower made the Sala Custodi available and the manuscripts were located there.

In January 1951 seven cases of good history books arrived at the Ambrosiana, the gift (1947) of Professor Ignazio Filippo Dengel of Innsbruck.

The time was opportune for the renewal of the interior life of the Institute. On July 16, 1951, having completed seventy years, Monsignor Giovanni Galbiati submitted his resignation as Prefect, "needless to say, not out of any desire for inert repose and not without the regret of many." Here as in the changing of the guard in 1924 we must distinguish between the official version and what really happened, which was rather complicated. The financial situation of the Ambrosiana was always fragile and precarious and in the years immediately following the Second World War the unforeseen devaluation made even daily bread uncertain. This can help explain certain questionable undertakings of Prefect Galbiati in those years, like the statues in "The Courtyard of the Great Minds." Here are found the St. Thomas Aquinas of the sculptor Marcello Gimondi,

the Plato of Luigi Orestano, the Paracelsus and Dante of Giannino Castiglioni, the Alexander Manzoni of Remo Riva, the Shakespeare of C. Brown, the Goethe of Walter Fleming and the Chateaubriand of E. Auricoste. To these were added, also as a result of initiatives of Galbiati, the the Hungarian poet Sandor Petofi in April, 1973 and the Roumanian prince Dimitri Cantemir. Even more unfortunate was the addition of certain Doctors *honoris causa*. Odd too were the gifts of works of art and codices. Moreover, Doctors had to make arrangements for outside teaching, and this inevitably entailed absences and consequent internal disputes. The eighty year old Monsignor Alessandro Bianchi was reduced to mendicancy: no one in the Piazza Fontana could help him and some help came to him from the charity of Cardinal Giovanni Mercati. The Prefect could respond meagerly or not at all to the repeated requests of poor and foreign students. To all this was added complaints from Rome; in the quiet halls of the Vatican the Cardinal librarian could not imagine that such tribulations were the daily lot of those in the Ambrosiana. For example, the present writer, elected Doctor on May 7, 1951, was provided the incredible annual stipend of three hundred thousand lire. For many years the congregation of Trustees was in fact reduced to a single person, Monsignor Vittore Maini who, because of the prolonged absences of Galbiati on the shores of Lago Maggiore, was often obliged to fulfill the role of prefect as well.

With the library reopened, the enormous damage sustained during the raid of August, 1943 became more obvious and it was only natural to seek someone to blame for it. In Rome the conclusion was too swiftly reached that the blame must fall primarily on the prefect who was then being criticized for according too much importance to the Pinacoteca, thus ignoring what Cardinal Federico had considered to be the primary point of his foundation. All these various accusations are unexpressed but discernible in the pages of the *Regolamento della Biblioteca Ambrosiana approvato da Pio XII*, printed by the Vatican Polyglot Press in 1948 and promulgated in Milan in November, 1949 when the congregation of Trustees was reconstituted. The baroque style alone suffices to prove that these pages were written by Cardinal Giovanni Mercati.

When Galbiati turned seventy in 1951 it was thought in Rome that his resignation could be asked for, all the more because he had surpassed the time (twenty-five years of service) necessary for a jubilee according to the Constitution, although the *Regolamento* of 1948 extended this to forty years. No one in

Rome really thought it was possible to get Galbiati to agree to step down; nonetheless, the authorities did not want to have recourse to the procedures for firing or removal to which, not by accident, the *Regolamento* of 1948 devoted pages. Recourse was thus made to a stratagem worth recording. In a letter dated June 11, 1951, the Secretary of State told Archbishop Schuster that the Holy Father, having learned of the gifts of pictures and codices made by Prefect Galbiati in Modena, Genoa and Milan without prior pontifical approval as prescribed by the bull *Creditam nobis* of Paul V of 1608, ordered the archbishop to declare to Galbiati that he had incurred the excommunication threatened by the Bull of 1608 but that the archbishop had received the faculty of absolving him from that sanction if within three days he would submit his immediate resignation in which case he would receive both a pension and lodging. This curious Roman document was communicated to Galbiati in Curia on July 6, 1951. It came as a genuine thrunderbolt if not from a sky entirely serene. Even Monsignore F. Mandelli wrote in 1980 that this Roman document "had been penned in an anonmolous way and could be contested from a juridical point of way."

Practically forced to resign, Galbiati *laudabiliter se subiecit* but for years he continued to write and make interventions to make it clear that in his own eyes the Roman move had been summarily unjust. It took twenty-eight months of negotiations in Rome and Milan to choose a successor. Finally on November 20, 1953 the Secretary of State communicated to Archbishop Schuster that the seventy-nine year old Carlo Castiglioni had been named prefect and that, Monsignor Agostinoi Saba having been named bishop of Tropea on August 25, 1953, the Reverend Enrico Galbiati had been named a new Doctor. Another Doctor, Monsignor Carlo Marcora, was named in December, 1953.

A dispassionate examination of these events leads to the conclusion that, as with Confalonieri's accusations against Gramatica in 1923, Mercatii's against Galbiati and the interventions of Saba in 1951 were only epiphenomena: the true cause of all these woes lay and lies in the impossibility of running in a decent way a cultural institution with structures more than three centuries old and without adequate means.

NOTES

For the Lucerne exhibition, see *Italienische Kunst: Kunstmuseum Luzern, 6 Juli bis 31 Oktober 1946.* Complete biographical information on G. Galbiati is in Miscellanea *Giovanni Galbiati,* Vol. 1, Milan, 1951, pp. XXXI-L: these pages are signed A(gostino) S(tocchetti), but were written by Galbiati. They were written after the events of 1951, which may explain their baroque bombast. An affectionate remembrance of Galbiati was published by Monsignor Federico Mandelli, *Profili di preti ambrosiani del Novecento,* Milan, 1980, pp. 193-207 (containing some errors of chronology as well as names). Moving and well informed pages were written by Agostino Stocchetti, *La Biblioteca Ambrosiana nella inaugurazione della sala Stocchetti,* Milan, 1975, pp. 51-65. The information I have given in the text was taken from handwritten letters of Galbiati laboriously retrieved from the mass of his still uncatalogued scribblings and have been kept to essentials. Among the lesser things may be remembered the series *I classici dell'amor sacro* initiated by Galbiati in the first months of 1946 to which more than sixty were asked to contribute and which came to a rapid and inglorious end. ---Around the ten statues of the "great spirits" beneath the porticos is found the *museo lapidario,* of which see the careful description by C. Marcora in *Archeologia e storia a Milano e nella Lombardia orientale,* editrice Cairoli, Como, 1980, pp. 177-289 (Amb. L. III.73). Monsignor Agostino Saba, Doctor of the Ambrosiana from 1930 to 1953, bishop of Nicotera and Tropea from '53 to '61, was translated to the see of Sassari, March 16, 1961, where he died January 19, 1962 (cf. *La Scuola Cattolica,* XC, 1962, p. 171).

XVII

A JUDGMENT OF THE COUNCIL OF STATE

In April 1956 the restoration of the old or Federician Sala being all but complete, furnished with new though still empty bookshelves, Archbishop Giovanni Battista Montini invited there the representatives of foreign nations participating in the *Fiera di Milano* for a solemn reception.

By date of December 11, 1956, the Council of State gave to the Ministry of Public Instruction (General Directorate of Libraries and Academies) who had requested it, the judgment ("*parere*") that the Ambrosian Library "could not be exempted, with respect to its rare and precious bibliographical material, from the law of June 1, 1939, n.1089, and in particular from the obligation to request, whenever there is an intention to get rid of something, government authorization as provided by article 26 of the same law." This judgment had been requested because the Prefect Castiglioni and Archbishop Montini had questioned the right of the Bibliographical Supervisor, Dr. Teresa Rogledi Manni, to intervene in the guardianship of the possessions of the Ambrosiana. In its judgment the Council of State recognized the Biblioteca Ambrosiana as "a patrimony with a cultural scope, endowed with a juridical personality by an ancient possession of state (prior to the civil code of 1865) and belonging to the category of *funzioni*."

Some irregularities in the Ambrosiana were subsequently made known to Superintendent Rogledi by the worthy Sir Maurizio Cogliati. This can be read in a communication from Dr. Rogledi to the Minister of Public Instruction on November 13, 1956. However both Prefect Castiglioni and the Archbishop of Milan were convinced that the information came to the Superintendant from the present writer. This explains, at least in part, the repeated apostolic visits of the years 1967-1972 and other tribulations which narrowly escaped becoming a third edition of the events of 1924 and 1951. What stopped this from happening, apparently, was the intervention at the Secretariat of State of Father Agostino Trape and of Monsignor Francesco Delpini the then president of the Trustees.

On June 13, 1959, the completion of the restoration and the inauguration of the new Fossati Bellani Sala were celebrated. Tullio Fossati Bellani, in order to honor in a lasting fashion the memory of his brother Vittorio wanted to prevent the dispersal of the library of travel books collected by the latter; he commissioned Antonio Pescarzoli to make a descriptive catalogue of it in three volumes and then gave the whole to the Ambrosiana, also providing for the preparation of a fitting room.

During the years C. Castiglioni directed the Ambrosiana, worthy additions were made to the series *Fontes Ambrosianae* initiated by G. Galbiati. First was a splendid reproduction of the *Ilias picta* edited by Dr. T. Burckhardt; then, in 1955, the *Cento Tavole del Codice Resta*, funded by the *Credito Italiano*; finally in 1957 the reproduction of the 60 plates of Pacioli, courtesy of the *Mediobanca*. There were besides significant acquisitions of volumes and collections of texts, reestablishing a tradition which had unfortunately been allowed to lapse for many years. Prefect Castiglioni published some books of wide circulation and in 1954 initiated a series *Memorie Storiche della Diocesi di Milano*. an annual volume of which appeared up to the last, Vol. XVI, in 1970. On the frontispece was the legend that these volumes were "deposited in the Ambrosian Library." Side by side with useful contributions on local history, the trustees were more than once too naive in accepting contributions of no value.

NOTES

Fuller information on the Fossati Bellani donation is found in the opusculum *Biblioteca Ambrosiana Milano 1609-1959*, published on the inauguration of the new Sala Fossati Bellani, June 13, 1959. In the introduction to the catalog, *I libri di viaggio e le guide della Raccolta L. V. Fossati Bellani*, Vol. I, Rome, 1957, don Giuseppe De Luca and Marino Moretti evoke the figure of Luigi Vittorio.

XVIII

NEW ACQUISITIONS

On May 12, 1960, the Ambrosiana celebrated the 350th anniversary of its founding by feting Pope John XXIII who in the years of his youth began his research into the age of St. Charles in these Federician halls. The Cardinal Archbishop G. B. Montini and Cardinal Tisserant took part along with the civil authorities. An exhibit of the Pizolpasso manuscripts was held in April, 1964 and, in November, an exposition of autographs and first editions of Cesare Beccaria's famous volume *Dei delitti e delle pene*. The Letters of Senator Alessandro Casati, one of the noblest figures of Italian politics in the first half of the 19th Century, came to the Ambrosiana at the end of 1964. The gift was made by Marchese Giovanni Incisa della Rocchetta, to whom the letters had been left by the senator's widow. In the Spring of 1965, during a visit to the Ambrosiana, Duke Tommaso Gallarati Scotti, announced his intention of leaving his personal archive to the Ambrosiana, his memoirs as well as his letters. In the years of his youth, the years of Rinnovamento, the duke had engaged in lengthy conversations in the corridors and porches of the library with don Achille Ratti. In a letter he wrote me from Bellagio in the summer of 1965 he said it seemed to him "that Providence truly accepts and aids my intention and brings together the writings of sharers in a spiritual enterprise that will find a secular haven in the beloved rooms of the Ambrosiana, free from base curiosity, objects only of serious research." The room dedicated to him was opened to a crowded reunion of authorities and friends on February 26, 1967. Just a few months before Duke Tommaso, his friend Uberto Pestalozza died and his children decided to give to the Ambrosiana his letters of the time of the Rinnovamento and his collection of books on the history of religions of which with filial devotion Dr. Cecilia Pestalozza made the catalog.

Pursuant to the will of her husband don Alfonso Falco, Prince Pio, the Princess Sveva Colonna gave the Ambrosiana the archives of Mombello d'Imbersago which contained six hundred cartons of documents as well as dozens of parchments, of particular interest the famous *rotulus* written at Ravenna at the end of the 7th Century. The Falco archive was located in the Sala Aureliana and the inauguration took place on October 6, 1969. Along with not a few other acquisitions, the Library was enriched by the books of Monsignor Carlo Bossi, of Monsignor Mario Busti, of Virginio Albarello, the gift of his son Franco, and of the notary Dr. Filippo Andronico, the gift of his widow.

As the crowning of a life wholly dedicated to study and teaching, Professor Agostino Stocchetti decided in 1970 to found next to the Milanese sanctuary of *Santa Maria presso San Celso* a library with the gift of his 12,000 volumes, in masssive walnut bookcases in two large and elegantly furnished rooms. With the participation of religious and civil authorities, it was inaugurated December 18, 1970 as a commemoration of the sacerdotal jubilee of Paul VI. But books alone do not a library make; one needs librarians too. A few months after the opening at San Celso, Professor Stocchetti was persuaded that his rich collection would be better located where it could be a useful instrument of students and scholars. Negotiations with the Ambrosiana were thus begun. The Oblate Fathers of San Celso graciously agreed to part with what they had so recently received and the Doctors and Conservators of the Ambrosiana gave their consent to the placement of the Stocchetti library in what once had been the chapel of the Angel Guardian and later came to be called the Sala Borromeo. It is now the Sala Stocchetti and not only contains a notable collection of modern books, Italian, Latin and French classics, works of history and art, but also enduringly commemorates a famous teacher of throngs of Milanese youth. Professor Agostino Stocchetti and his brother Giovanni also donated the magnificent glass door facing the piazza San Sepolcro with its wrought iron work and windows whose historic design is of the school of Fra Agnelico. Cardinal Archbishop G.

Colombo, patron and moderator of the Ambrosiana Library, having consulted the colleges of Doctors and Conservators, conferred on Professor Agostino Stocchetti the title of Doctor of the Ambrosian Library honoris causa on June 20, 1975.

The Ambrosiana Microfilming Project should also be regarded as an enrichment of the ancient Federican library. Under the direction of Professor Astrik L. Gabriel of its Medieval Institute, the University of Notre Dame, Notre Dame, Indiana, after many years of work completed the microfilming of all the Ambrosiana codices. The idea of this project had been proposed to the president of the university, Father Theodore Hesburgh, by the then Cardinal Montini during a 1960 visit to Notre Dame. These microfilms represent a significant part of the holdings of the Medieval Institute which developed into a notable research center under Dr. Gabriel's direction and Father Hesburgh's encouragement. Dr. Ralph McInerny, Michael P. Grace Professor of Medieval Studies and current Director of the Medieval Institute, is directing the preparation of a summary catalogue of the microfilmed manuscripts by Dr. Susan Wool. with the aid of funds from the Mellon Foundation and the National Endowment for the Humanities. Under a grant from the Kress Foundation, Drs. Louis Jordan and Robert Coleman are cataloguing the Mary Davis Renaissance Drawings with the counsel and wisdom of Professor Gabriel ever at their disposal. The link between the Biblioteca Ambrosiana and The Medieval Institute of the University of Notre Dame, forged by Drs. Gabriel and Paredi, grows ever stronger.

NOTES

On the Casati letters, see *Il Corriere della Sera* of December 17, 1965. On the Gallarati Scotti archive, see *Il Corriere della Sera* of February 16, 1967. On the origins and the scope of the Ambrosiana Microfiliming Project, see A. L. Gabriel, *A Summary Catalogue of Microfilms of One Thousand Scientific Manuscripts in the Ambrosiana Library*, Notre Dame Indiana, 1968.

XIX

RENOVATION OF THE PINACOTECA

There have been notable additions to the Pinacoteca during recent years as well. In 1959 Commandante Attilio Brivio made a donation of a group of paintings of various schools some of which have been securely attributed to famous artists, others have still to be studied but all the same derive from schools and workshops of the great tradition.

The Pinacoteca Ambrosiana, by the gift of Count Vincenzo Negroni Prati Morosini, received in 1962 a new group of works of art: four large portraits by Francesco Hayez, a Procaccini; a Nuvolone; a beautiful portrait of Napoleon, the work of Andrea Appiani, a sketch by F. Hayez and a fine table with marble top. Moreover Count Negroni provided in his will that the Ambrosiana should be represented in the Foundation he wished his heirs to form.

The courageous task of renovating the Pinacoteca became ever more urgent. Both Ratti's reorganization of 1906 and Galbiati's of 1932, hewed to the plans made in the 17th and 18th centuries: long rows of pictures, one next to the other, and hung from floor to ceiling as in *La Galleria dell'arciduca Leopoldo* of painted by Teniers junior, where thirty-five pictures on a single wall can be seen, eight more on the side of a cabinet and seven resting on the floor: fifty paintings in one place. So too the

Galleria del Cardinal Valenti of G. P. Pannini which can be seen at Capodimonte. Many masterpieces of the first rank were surrounded by crowds of things of dubious value in the Ambrosiana picture galleries. The lighting had never been adequate and of heating there was none at all.

Long nurtured hopes were finally realized thanks to the intelligent and generous help of Signora Giulia Devoto Falck who brought together at her home on March 1, 1965 myself and Gian Alberto Dell'Acqua, inviting us to consult with the architect Luigi Caccia Dominioni concerning the restoration and rearrangement of the Pinacoteca. In order to get the project immediately under way, it seemed advisable to concentrate oon the area surrounding the ancient cortile on the second floor. Furthermore, only paintings of the highest value, that is, the original Federican nucleus and the best of subsequent donations, not the whole collection, should be shown. December 7, 1966, the Pinacoteca Ambrosiana was reopened to the applause and delight of authorities and friends.

The renovation plans called for the abolishing of the old drawings and prints room. In compensation it seemed advisable to provide for the restoration of the drawings and prints and then to rearrange them in a convenient and secure way. This project became possible because of the help of the Cassa di Risparmio delle Provincie Lombarde and the interest of its president, Professor Giordano Dell'Amore. The Ambrosiana found expert and qualified collaborators in this difficult task in the *Staatliche Graphische Sammlung* in Munich, Bavaria, especially its director, Dr. Bernhard Degenhart. A small valuable group of primitive Italian drawings by German artists was exhibited in Munich from November 1967 to January 1968.

A full account of the renovation of the Pinacoteca must include thanks to the patronage of the Cassa di Risparmio delle Provincie Lombarde. On January 20, 1968, Professor Giordano Dell'Amore published the splendid volume *L'Ambrosiana*. Although up to 1966 the average annual number of visitors to the Pinacoteca did not surpass 6000, after the renovation the number of visitors per year jumped to an average of 30,000.

NOTES

A hint of the various descriptions of the Federician gallery (1625, 1672, 1860, 1895, 1907, 1932, 1951, 1957) can be found in the catalog *La Pinacoteca Ambrosiana* prepared by A. Falchetti, Neri Pozza, 1969.

XX

THE THEFTS OF 1968

The moving of some hundreds of pictures during work on the gallery in 1965-66 enabled "someone" to take the little engraving "Daniel in the Lion's Den" (28 x 38cm) by Jan Bruegel. It was on display briefly in the piazzetta Bossi in Milan without anyone suspecting its provenance, in an antiquarian gallery which sold it to the Newhouse Galleries in New York. It ended in the home of Mr. John Lowenthal. He, familiar with our guidebooks, wrote asking about our Bruegel and soon realized that his was ours. After discrete negotiations, the engraving was returned in 1966 though we were still in ignorance as to the identity of that "someone." It was the Milanese gallery that was hurt in the matter since they were obliged to return it to us without compensation and to bear the burden of their imprudent acquisition. The return was simply good luck owing to the honesty of an American who, had he kept the engraving hidden, would certainly have prevented us from ever recovering it. The strange episode was the first of several woes.

Later it emerged that the "someone" alluded to above was an employee who had been taken on as a result of the charitable insistence of one of the Conservators. He was let go in September, 1965 (after the theft of the engraving) in order to take a job at the library of San Fedele. In April, 1968, he asked to come back and we rehired him, little suspecting that a nefarious calculation lay behind his request. He had been under constant pressure from those to whom he had given the engraving in 1965; they wanted him to go back to the Ambrosiana so as to be able to steal other things. He was rehired in April 1968 and within three months I was informed by the police that in the circles frequented by him there was talk of the sale of our codices and drawings; the thefts were blamed on our employee although the police knew only his baptismal and not his surname. At the beginning of September 1968 it was noticed that an illuminated codex (c. 20. inf.: *Delphili somnium*) was missing. A survey of all manuscripts and incunabula was called for and it was discovered that four codices and fifteen incunabala were missing. With a good deal of shrewdness the guilty one was persuaded to confess; on September 17 our employee Anselmo Mancarella admitted that he was responsible for the theft of the engraving in 1965 and of the other things in 1968.

Another incredible instance took place at the end of October, 1968. Filming the last pages of the *Codice Atlantico* before taking it to Grottaferrata for restoration, we noticed that a double folio was missing (Piumati NN. 342 and 343). Mancarella admitted this stupid theft to the police and after a frenetic hunt the double folio was brought back from Lugano to Milan on November 13. By underhanded methods, our declaration at police headquarters found its way into the newspapers. There followed a flood of publicity, much of it sensational, in both the domestic and foreign press, along with solemn and plangent laments of a certain predator on the decadence of Italian breed of librarian (as if foreign libraries were immune to theft). Endless recriminations descended from both sacred and secular superiors combined on the head of your humble servant and no one thought to congratulate the police for their prompt recovery in a matter of months of all the codices and almost all the incunabula.

Woes of another kind arose in 1968-69 because of another employee who had been hired at the insistence of the first apostolic visitator without the information that the man had been previously convicted. Similar misfortunes came at the time to other Milanese cultural institutions such as the Roccolta Bertarelli, the Poldi Pezzoli, the Braidense, but those at the Ambrosiana received more clamorous and prolonged publicity. Indeed, long after the matter had been settled, there were those who would raise the issue again from time to time. First there was *Il Borghese* on May 3 and 10, 1970; then *Il Giorno* on

December 31, 1971 and *Il Corriere della Sera* on September 20, 1972 and *Il Giorno* again December 17, 1973. Looking back from the distance of a decade on these recurrent and insinuating stories, inane and venomous as they were, it is difficult not to suspect some tortured mind with an ulterior objective he luckily failed to achieve.

Mention must be made of some recent munificent gifts. In 1966 Pope Paul VI came to the aid of the Ambrosiana with a generous donation. The Banco Popolare di Milano in 1968-69 provided for restoration work in the reading room and the installation of curtains; thanks to a donation from the Credito Artigiano new metal bookshelves were installed in the Sala Fagnani. These shelves, which the apostolic visitator wanted despite the wishes of the Doctors, received criticism. Dr. Raffaele Mattioli of the Banca Commerciale Italiani made possible the publication of the catalogue of the incunabula (the first volume appeared in 1972) and the catalogue of Arabic codices (the first volume of which appeared in 1975). In 1973, the Cassa di Risparmio delle Provincie Lombarde, commemorating the 150th anniversary of its founding, gave the extraordinarily generous gift of 50 million lire to the Ambrosiana for the purpose of adding another room to the Pinacoteca. For some years the *Fondazione Ercole Varzi* has provided funds for the restoration of Ambrosiana codices which are particularly valuable because of their illuminations. With the aid of old and new friends, the Conservators succeeded in getting under way the reorganization of the Villa Pogliaghi on Sacro Monte in Varese and in 1974-75 provided for the restoration of San Carlo in Arona. In 1974, La Centrale Finanziaria Generale put at the disposal of the Ambrosiana the means to create electronically consulting indices of 12,000 parchments in our library thereby making them accessible to distant scholars.

NOTES

From among the many articles in newspapers and reviews on these matters mention may be made of the informed account of Ricciotti Lazzero in *Epoca*, November 24, 1968, though even his contains imprecisions and fantastic embellishments.

XXI

THE NEW NORMS

Three successive apostolic delegates came from Rome for the purpose of updating the 17th Century constitution of the Ambrosiana: from 1967 to 1970 Monsignor Maggioni; from November 1970 to September 1972, Father Alfonso Raes, S.J.; finally from September 1972 to July 1973, Father Agostino Trape. It was the third visitator who was able to get to the substance of the problem. Father Trape himself understood and made the responsible authorities understand that before everything else the Ambrosiana needed the means with which to operate. At the conclusion of these visits the Holy See decided to turn responsibility, organizational, administrative and governing, of the library over to the Archdiocese of Milan *pro tempore* and issued new Norms which came into force January 1, 1974. That year was the 16th centenary of the election of Saint Ambrose as bishop of Milan. In support of Cardinal Archbishop Giovanni Colombo as he assumed the new and heavy administrative responsibilities for the Ambrosiana, the Banco Ambrosiano gave assurance of lasting and constant help. A bilingual edition of all the writings (*opera omnia*) of Saint Ambrose was begun in 1974, one more fruit of the celebration. The initiative was backed by Cardinal Giovanni Colombo, who entrusted the publication to the *Citta Nuova Editrice* and the editorial responsibility to the Biblioteca Ambrosiana. Two new temporary Doctors were added for this purpose. The publication was made possible by a gift from the engineer Dr. Aldo Bonacossa (1885-1974) which became the basis of the *Fondazione sant'Ambrogio per la cultura cristiana*. The first volume of the *Opera Omnia* was presented to the public in the Sala di Raffaello on January 16, 1978; next to Cardinal Colombo were the Honorable Mario Pedini, Minister of Cultural Affairs, and Professor Francesco Sisinni, Director General of the Central Office for Libraries.

In 1978, Professor Marco Valsecchi, talented art critic for many years, first in *Il Giorno* and then in *Il Giornale Nuovo*, gave to the Ambrosiana, "so that it might be accessible to everyone," his valuable collection of art books and books in the history of art. There were more than five thousand titles; many more were donated by his sisters Angelian and Antonia after his death on December 17. 1980.

Another important addition to the Pinacoteca came from the Cav. Gr. Cr. Aldo Croff who, in January 1981, as a memorial of his Angelina, donated the huge panel by Baldassarre Estense, *Il Transito della Vergine*. (See the *Enciclopedia Treccani*, Vol. 5, 1930, p. 951).

In recent years, centers of civil authority like the Regione Lombardia, the Commune di Milano, and the Provinicial Administration, recognizing the public role of the institution, have begun to allocate funds for the Ambrosiana too, though still far from recovering the needs of normal functioning even when reduced to the vital minimum.

These pages bear the title "history," not because they pretend to be an exhaustive account of the events of three centuries, but only for the sake of brevity. I have relied on my introduction to *Ambrosiana*, published by the Cassa di Risparmio delle Provincie Lombarde in 1967 and I have used not a few passages written by Achille Ratti in the *Guida Sommaria* published in 1907 as well as the brochure *L'Ambrosiana* written by Luigi Gramatica in 1923. My first aim has been to keep alive the memory of those who have been benefactors of the Ambrosiana. There are many reasons to want to do this, but the following is the principal one: Cardinal Federico Borromeo's venerable institution has ever enjoyed the esteem and affection of the Milanese, both the poor and the wealthy, who see in it a means of culture, of civic education, always strong and alive.

NOTES

The norms in force since January 1, 1974 came from Rome in typescript. Perhaps a period of experimentation was envisaged prior to given them a definitive and printed form. One thing is certain: like Muratori in the 17th Century the librarians of today have more than one reason to lament "the rules of this library."

Information and a bibliography of the *Prefects* of the Ambrosiana have been published by C. Castiglioni in *Miscellanea G. Galbiati*, II, Milan, 1951, pp. 399-429; of the *Doctors* (with many errors and lacunae) in *Memorie Storiche della diocesi di Milano*, II, Milan, 1955, pp. 9-71. On the Ambrosiana in general, see the article of L. Gramatica in the *Enciclopedia Italiana Treccani*, Vol. II, 1929, pp. 802; the bibliographical bulletin of A. Saba in *Aevum*, VI, Milan, 1932, pp.531-620; the articles of Galbiati in *Enciclopedia Cattolica*, Vol. I, Rome, 1948, 1014-1019; the bibliegraphical information in Galbiati, *Itinerario dell'Ambrosiana*, Milan, 1951, pp. 66-92; A. Hobson, *Great Libraries*, London, 1970, pp. 186-195, as well as the various other publications mentioned in the foregoing pages.

CATALOGUES OF THE AMBROSIAN LIBRARY

I. Manuscripts

1) *Hebrew*: C. Bernheimer, *Codices hebraici Bybliothecae Ambrosianae*, Florentiae, 1933 (Cons. F. VI. 5); *Hebraica Ambrosiana*, by Aldo Luzzatto and Luisa Mortara Ottolenghi, Il Polifilo, Milan, 1972 (Cons. F. VI. 45).

2) *Greek*: A. Martini et D. Bassi, *Catalogus cod. graecorum Bibl. Ambrosianae*, tom. I-II, Milan, 1906 (Cons. F. VII. 20-21).

3) *Latin*: There is as yet no catalogue of all the Latin manuscripts but only indexes and catalogues of the following groups:

A) Hagiographical materials: *Catalogus codicum hagiographicorum latinorum Bibl. Ambrosianae Analecta Bollandiana*, XI, Brussels, 1892, pp. 205-368 (Cons. F. VII. 17); for Greek hagiographia in the Ambrosiana manuscripts, see Halkin, BHG, 1957 (Cons. M. VII. 47. a. b. c.) and the *Supplements Ambrosiens a la Bibl. Hagiogr. Graeca* in *Analecta Bollandiana*, LXXII, 1954, pp. 325-342 (Cons. M. VIII. 72)

B) Ancient manuscripts: E. A Lowe, *Codices Latini Antiquiores*, Part III, Italy: Ancona-Novara, Oxford, 1938, nn. 304-365 (Cons. O. VII. 26). A minute description from a paleographical point of view is given of 67 codices and fragments of codices. A list of the palimpsest manuscriupts in the Ambrosiana has been published by Lowe, "Codices rescripti," in *Melanges Tisserant*, Vol. V, Vatican City, 1964, pp. 67-113 (Amb. D.VIII.86): 889 folios have now been indexed by Dr. P. F. Fumagalli.

C) Bobbio manuscripts: P. Collura, *Studi paleografici: La precarolina e la carolina a Bobbio*, Milan, 1943 (Cons. F. VI. 22);"Rassegna di studi bobbiesi del dopoguerra 1943-1955," in *Aevum*, 30, 1956, p. 246 ff.

D) Latin Pinelli manuscripts: A. Rivolta, *Catalogo dei codici Pinelliani (latini) dell'Ambrosiana*, Milan, 1933 (Cons. F. VII. 18). A provisory index of the Greek Pinelli manuscripts has been prepared by Dr. Marcella Grendler. Cf. Cons. F. VII. 21 bis.

E) Pizolpasso manuscripts: cf. A. Paredi, *La Biblioteca del Pizolpasso*, Milan, 1961 (Cons. F. VII.
26 bis).

F) Humanistic: Cf. P. O. Kristeller, *Iter Italicum*, I, Leiden, 1963, pp. 277-350; II, Leiden, 1967, pp. 529-36 (Cons. F. VII. 28, 1-2).

4) *Geographical*: P. Revelli, *I Codici ambrosiani dicontenuto geografico*, Milan, 1929 (Cons. F. VI. 1).

5) *Illuminated*: A. Mai, *Iliadis fragmenta*, Milan, 1819, p. viii ff. in notes; A. Saba in *Aevum*, VI, Milan, 1932, pp. 596-597; M. L. Gengaro, F. Leoni, G. Villa, *Codici decorati e miniati del'Ambrosiana: ebraici e greci*, Milan, 1959 (Cons. F. VI. 33A); M. L. Gengaro, G. Villa Guglielminetti, *Inventario dei cod. decorati e miniati della Bibl. Ambr. (sec. VII-XIII)*, Florence, 1968 (Cons. F. VII. 24); Renata Cipriani, *Codici miniati dell'Ambrosiana*, Neri Pozza editore, 1968 (Cons. F. VI. 40); *Miniature Lombarde*, edizione Cassa di Risparmio delle Provincie Lombarde, Milan, 1970 (S.R.C. VII. 26). For the miniatures in the *libri d'ore*, see G. Marcora, *Ilibri d'ore della Biblioteca Ambrosiana*, Milan, 1973 (I. Hie. A. IX. 20).

6) *Musical*: there is the partial and incomplete catalogue of G. Cesari, *Catalogo Opere Musicali: Milano, Bibl. Ambros.*, Parma, 1910-II (Cons. F. VII. 2). The publication of a complete catalogue by Dr. Maria Angela Dona is anticipated.

7) *Arabic*: G. De Hammer Purgstall, *Catalogo dei codici arabi, persiani e turchi della Bibl. Ambr.* in *Bibliotesa Italiana*, 94, 1839, Milan, 1839, p. 22 ff, p. 322 ff. This comprises 340 codices, practically the whole of the old collection (Cons. F. VII. 25); E. Griffini, *Catalogo dei manoscritti arabi di nuovo fondo della Biblioteca Ambrosiana*, Vol. I (the only one to appear), codices 1-475, Rome, 1910-19 (Cons. F. VII. 19) Of this new collection which came to the Ambrosiana from Yemen in 1909 and 1914, the

Fondo Caprotti, some 1790 manuscripts, mainly miscellaneous, there exists another partial catalogue: E. Griffini, "Die juengste Ambrosianische Sammlung arabisher Handschriften," in *Zeitschriftdes Deutschen Morgenlaendischen Gesellschaft*, Vol. 64, Leipzig, 1915, pp. 63-88: this describes 39 codices (Cons. F. VII. I9). The first volume of a new catalogue of the arabic manuscripts appeared in 1975: *Catalogue of the Arabic Manuscripts in the Biblioteca Ambrosiana*, by Oscar Lofgren and Renato Traini, Vol. I: *Antico Fondo and Medio Fondo*, Neri Pozza Editore (Cons. F. VI. 51). In 1981 the second volume appeared covering 800 more manuscripts of the A, B, C and D series of the *Nuovo Fondo* (Cons. F. VI. 66).

8) *Armenian*: F. Macler, "Notices des manuscripts armeniens de la Bibl. Ambros.," in *Journal Asiatique*, settembre-ottobre, 1913. Six codices (V.P. 23070).

9) *Ethiopian*: S. Grebaut,"Catalogue des manuscripts ethiopiens de la Bibl. Ambr.," in *Revue de l'Orient chretien*, t. IX, III serie, 1933-34, pp. 3-32 (7 codices); E. Galbiati, "I mss. etiopici dell'Ambrosiana," in *Studi in onore di C. Castiglioni*, Milan, 1957, pp. 337-353 (Cons. F. VI. 32).

10) *Syriac*: J. B. Chabot, "Inventaire des fragments de manuscrits syriaques conserves a la B.A. a Milan," in *Museon*, 49, 1936, pp. 39-54 (S.P. 10, 34).

11) *Scientific*: A. L. Gabriel, *A Summary Catalogue of Microfilms of One Thousand Scientific Manuscripts in the Ambrosiana Library*, Notre Dame, 1968 (Cons. F. VII. 30); J. Agrimi, *Tecnica e scienza nella cultura medievale*, Florence, 1976, pp. 74-184 (Cons. F.VII. 29); F. Bazzi, *Catalogo dei mss. e degli incunaboli di interesse medico-naturalistico dell'Ambrosianae della Braidense*, Milan, 1961 (Cons. F. VII. 1 bis).

12) *Other Groupings*: Dante manuscripts, French, Gothic, Irish, liturgical, are often cited in A. Saba's bibliographical bulletin in *Aevum*, VI, Milan, 1932 (Riv. 174) It should be noted that the Ambrosiana does not have (and never did have) the d'Annunzio manuscripts of Alcione; what Saba writes (op. cit., p. 558) does not correspond with the truth; the poet made a promise on the occasion of his visit to the Ambrosiana on March 6, 1926, of which a record is found in his own handwriting in a specially bound volume of Susio (S.P. II. 73). For the Beccaria collection, see *Catalogo della Libreria Villa Pernice*, Milan, 1890 (Cons. F. VII. 14); *Mostra commemorativa di Cesare Beccaria*, Milan, 1964, pp. 181-208 (Cons. F. VI. 58). For the Salvioni collection, see Paolo A. Fare, *I Manoscritti T. inf. della Bibl. Ambrosiana*, Milan, 1968 (Conf. F. VII. 39). The Enrico Molteni letters are in mss. Z.267-268

Sup. The Ilarione Rancati letters are in five Sussido manuscripts, B256, B266, F 2, M 74, M 75

13) Mention must also be made of the *Indice inventario dell'epistolario di San Carlo Borromeo (Cons. F. VII. 1), the portion of which is contained in the Ambrosiana having been compiled by the Rev. Dr. Adolfo Rivolta; 24 volumes of minutes and letters of St. Charles (P. 1-25 inf.), chronologically arranged first by Prefect L. Gramatica and now by Monsignor A. Fustella; the Schedario* (in 27 boxes) of those corresponding with St. Charles; and finally the "Inventario delle lettere indirizzate al cardinale Federico Borromeo" published in the volume *Card. Federico Borromeo, Indice delle lettere a lui dirette conservate all'Ambrosiana*, Milan, 1960 (Cons. F. VI. 34).

14) For the Bonomelli letters the manuscript *Inventario* and *Indice dei corrispondenti* can be consdulted; there is a manuscript *Inventario* of the letters of Alessandro Casati; for the Falco archive, see *Inventario dell—archivio Falco Pio di Savoia*, edited by Ugo Fiorina, Neri Pozza, 1980 (Cons. F. VI. 64). A summary *Inventario analitico* of the letters of Tommaso Gallarati Scotti was made in 1966 and an *Elenco dei* Corrispondenti is in preparation.

15) Of all the manuscripts in the Ambrosiana there is the ancient catalogue (*Manuductio* ...) in three volumes, to which a fourth volume has been added: *Appendix ad manud.* (Cons. F. VII. 3-6). It has now been transcribed on sheets of standard international size which are in a notebook kept in the *Sala di lettura*.

Inventario Ceruti

A summary description of all the manuscripts which came to the Ambrosiana to the end of the last century is contained in the 33 manuscript volumes of the *Inventario Ceruti*, named after Antonio Ceruti, the Doctor of the Ambrosiana who complied it. Monsignor Antonio Ceruti, born in Milan on April 11, 1830, died in Cernobbio May 20, 1919, entered the Ambrosiana in August, 1863. He was a prodigious worker and a bit of a character. On his death bed, after receiving the consolations of religion, he cried out, "Great God, to die so young!" He was 88 years old. A benevolent grouch, he left a not inconsiderable sum to his heirs (350,000 1911 Lire), among them the Ambrosiana and the Royal Lombard Institute of Science and Literature. The *Inventario Ceruti*, despite its imperfections, remains a useful instrument of research. In recent years (1973-1979), a photographic reproduction in five volumes has been published by Edizioni Etimar of Trezzano sul Naviglio.

Of the other manuscripts, either overlooked or come to the Ambrosiana in recent years, Sir Maurizio Cogliati, who has worked fifty years in the Ambrosiana, has compiled careful inventories, a list of which follows. They are given as continuations of the 33 volumes of the Ceruti:

Vol. 34 Provisory and partial catalogue of the Fondo Sussidio: A. 1-294; B.137-246; C. 65-75 and 102; D. 6 and 141; G. 252; H. 140; I. 63 and 65; L. 156.

Vol. 35 Fondo Trotti (formerly Q 130 sup.) Partial inventory (see Vol. 48).

Vol. 36 Sussidio A. 1-331.

Vol. 37 Sussidio B. 1-376.

Vol. 38 Sussidio C. 1-152.

Vol. 39 Sussidio D. 1-142.

Vol. 40 Sussidio E. 1-67; Sussidio F. 1-70.

Vol. 41 Sussidio G. 1-384.

Vol. 42 Sussidio H. 1-163.

Vol. 43 Sussidio I. 1-148.

Vol. 44 Sussidio L. 1-167.

Vol. 45 Sussidio M. 1-139.

Vol. 46 Sussidio N. 1-153; N. VIII. 9-10; 0.VIII.13-14; P. VIII.1-7; S. VIII. 1-13; T. 1-36: Ex libris Lodovico Pogliaghi.

Vol. 47 Sussidio: S.Q.$I. 1-36; S.Q.$II. 1-57.

Vol. 48 Sussidio: Trotti 1-573 (see Vol. 35)

Vol. 49 I inf. 262-440 (continuation of Vol. 11 of Ceruti).

Vol. 50 $51-101 sup. (continuation of Vol. 33 of Ceruti); 205-263 sup. (continuation of Vol. 33 of Ceruti); E. 90-100 inf. (continuation of Vol. 7 of Ceruti); G. 309-313 inf. (continuation of Vol. 9 of Ceruti); H. 270-281 inf. (continuation of Vol. 10 of Ceruti).

Vol. 51 A.189-216 sup. (continuation of Vol. 12 of Ceruti); B. 175-187 sup. (continuation of Vol. 13 of Ceruti); H. 122-126 sup. (continuation of Vol. 19 of Ceruti); I 124-134 sup. (continuation of Vol. 20 of Ceruti); M. 100-112 sup. (continuation of Vol. 22 of Ceruti).

Vol. 52 Q. 250-310 sup. (continuation of Vol. 24 of Ceruti).

Vol. 53 Q. 131-140 sup. (continuation of Vol. 26 of Ceruti); S. 161-165 sup. (continuation of Vol. 28 of Ceruti); V. 37-90 sup]. (continuation of Vol. 30 of Ceruti).

Vol. 54 N.I. 1-22 inf. (nn. 1-134 included). The Rev. Achille Varisco collection (July 1, 1909).

Vol. 55 A. 277-367 inf. (continuation of Vol. 1 of Ceruti).

Vol. 56 Z. 261-519 sup. (continuation of Vol. 32 of Ceruti).

Vol. 57 Archivio Cesare Cantu: R. 1-23 inf. Vol. I (foll. 1-210).

Vol. 58 Archivio Cesare Cantu: R. 23-52 inf., Vol. II (foll. 211-361).

Vol. 59 Archivio Cesare Cantu: R. 52-69 inf., Vol. III (foll. 362-480).

Vol. 60 Archivio Cesare Cantu: R. 69-103 inf., Vol. IV (foll. 481-631) and a list of the documents in the Archivio Cantu (S.P. 29 bis).

Vol. 61 R. 104-269 inf.

Vol. 62 S. 1-230 inf.

Vol. 63 X. 279-348 inf.

Vol. 64 L. 122-132 sup. (continuation of Vol. 21 of Ceruti). T. 160 bis-167 sup. A list of noble Milanese families (Raffaele Fagnani). (Continuation of Vol. 29 of Ceruti).

Vol. 65 L. 1-44 inf.; M. 1-22 inf.; N.I. 1-108 inf.; N.II. 1-15 inf.

Vol. 66 O. 1-47 inf.; P. 1-15 inf. Minutes of letters of St. Charles Borromeo and an index to them ; Q. 1-43 inf.; Y. 1-24 inf. Letters of General Giuseppe Sirtori and of General Vincenzo Giordano Orsini.

Vol. 67 Letters of various authors from various codices: M. 98 sup. to Giulio Carcano; R. 122 inf. from Giulio Carcano to his daughter and to his wife; R. 129 inf. from Maria Carcano; L. 125 sup. to Giulio Carcano A-L); L. 126 sup. to Giulio Carcano (M-Z); L. 127 sup. from Giuseppe Pecis; L. 122 sup. to Felice Bellotti (A-H); L. 123 sup. to Felice Bellotti (L-P); L. 124 sup. to Felice Bellotti (R-Z); L. 125 sup. Bellotti family letters; R. 246 inf. to Pietro Mazzucchelli; R. 203 inf. (insert n. 5) to Carlo Morbio; R. 242 inf. to Giov. Batt. Branca; S.Q. $I. 36 to Bernardo Gatti and others; G. 136 sussidio, manuscripts and letters of Giov. Rasori; Y. 178 bis sup. from L. A. Muratori to the Prefect G. A. Sassi; Z. 208-212 sup., to G. A. Sassi; B. 63 sussidio, to Count Giulio Porro; D. 501 inf. to Father Ant. Panvinio, Augustinian; S.Q. $II.51, to Cardinal Francesco Albani; T. 183 sup, from the Duke of Savoy, Emmanuele Filiberto; & 162 sup., to Francesco Alessio Fiori, former Jesuit; Z. 390 sup, from Baron Giovanni Labus and letters of General Camillo Vacani.

Vol. 68 T. 125-142 sup. Letters to Father Isidoro Bianchi, Camaldolese; Y. 148-154 sup., Letters to Father Paolo Frisi, Barnabite; Z. 1-104 inf., Various manuscripts ; Z. 1-69 inf., Ancient catalogues of the Ambrosiana Library.

Vol. 69 A. Giuseppi Bossi collection (summary inventory).

B. Autograph letters in alphabetical order: Aschenbach-Botero S.P. II.263; Boschi-Buonarroti S.P. II. 264; Caccia-Cusani

S.P. II.265; De Bono-Fruehwirth S.P. II.266; Gagliardi-Guanella S.P. II.267; Hammer-Muzzi S.P. II.268; Mercati-Mussi S.P. II.269; Nogara-Possenti S.P. II. 270; Radini-Rusconi S.P. II.271; Sacchi-Schuster S.P. II.272; Taschi-Zanella S.P. II.273.

C. Various autograph letters S.P. II.274; Various letters from the time of Cardinal Federico Borromeo S.P. II.275; Letters and documents (gift of Monsignor Carlo Castiglioni) S.P. II.276; Letters to G. A. Sassi S.P. II. 277; Various letters, S.P. II.278; Various letters (to G. Forziati) S.P. II.279; Various letters S.P. II.280; Various letters S.P. II.281.

D. Felice Bellotti miscellany S.P. II. 286; Letters to Cardinal Agostino Cusani S.P. II.288; autograph letters from the Varisco collection, S.P. II.289.

E. A.367 inf. Various letters (continuation of Vol. 1 of Ceruti).

Vol. 70 Inventory catalogue of the manuscripts and printed works located in the Sala Prefetto (5 S.P.) with card index in alphabetical order.

Vol. 71 Inventory catalogue of the archives of Monsignor Geremia Bonomelli, Bishop of Bergamo (1871-1914) with alphabetical index.

Vol. 72 Inventory catalogue of the letters of the Count and Senator Alessandro Casati with alphabetical index.

Vol. 73 Analytic inventory catalogue of the archives of Duke Tommaso Gallarati Scotti, compiled by Dr. Nicola Raponi and Sir M. Cogliati.

Vol. 74-78 G. 138-158 and 265 inf. Inventory-Catalogue of letters addressed to Cardinal Federico Borromeo in the possession of the Ambrosiana.

Vol. 79-85 Inventories of miscellaneous codices.

Vol. 86-87 Inventory of drawings.

Vol. 88 Topographical catalogue of the books located in the Sala Prefetto.

Vol. 89 Topographical catalogue of the volumes in the Sala Rosa.

Vol. 90 Inventory of the Ceruti Volumes.

II. Noteworthy Parchments

The collection contains some 12,000 documents, the most ancient of which dates from the year 819; Alessandro Bianchi, a Doctor of the Ambrosiana, compiled the *Schedario* (Index) of these in alphabetical order as well as the *Inventario Regesto delle Pergamene* (inventory of parchments) in twelve manuscript

Volumes (Amb. H. VII.21-32). In Volume XII, pp. 447-51 is found a list of illuminated parchments. The Bianchi registers have been electronically reproduced by *La Centrale Finanziaria Generale* (Piazzetta M. Bossi 2, Milano), from whom microfilms and microfiches can be obstained by applying to Data Management S. p. A., Viale Eginardo 29, Milano.

III. Drawings

There are in the Ambrosiana numerous miscellaneous collections which have been partly put in order by Dr. Giorgio Fubini. Slides and photographs of the drawings make up the Mary Davis Collection at the University of Notre Dame. A catalogue of the drawings is under way there thanks to a grant of the Samuel Kress Foundation.

S. P. 1 Leonardo da Vinci, *Codice Atlantico*.

S.P. 6 Luca Paciolo, *De divina proportione*.

S.P. 6 bis Petrus Pictor (Piero della Francesca), *De Prospectiva pingendi*.

S.P. armadio 10, n. 33, Bramantino (Bartolomeo Suardi), drawings of ancient Rome.

F. 210-212 inf. Flowers and herbs, 17th Century.

F. 213 inf. Fortification plans and fortified cities, 17th century.

F. 214 inf. Pisanello (26 drawings). Cf. *Disegni del Pisanello e di Maestri del suo tempo*, catalogue of an exhibit, prepared by Annegrit Schmitt, Neri Pozza, 1966 (Cons. F. VII.37).

F. 215-219 inf. Botanical gardens, 18th century.

F. 220 inf. Various figure drawings, landscapes, etc.

F. 221 inf. Ancient pictures of Rome (Grimaldi), 17th century.

F. 225-226 inf. Colored drawings of plants, herbs and flowers, 17th century.

F. 227-229 inf. Copies of sacred and symbolic pictures in Rome, 17th century.

F. 320 inf. Drawings by A. D. Gabbiani, 18th century.

F. 231 inf. Drawings, 17th century.

F. 232 inf. Drawings, 17th century.

F. 233 inf. Drawings, 17th century.

F. 234 inf. Drawings, 17th-18th centuries.

F. 235 inf. Drawings, 17th and 18th centuries.

F. 236 inf. Drawings, 17th and 18th centuries.

F. 237 inf. Drawings, 17th century.

F. 238 inf. Drawings, 17th century.

F. 243 inf. Details of Carracci's ceiling in the Farnese Palace in Rome.

F. 245 inf. Drawings, 16th century.

F. 246 inf. Drawings, 16th century.

F. 249 inf. Drawings by P. Rubens and Michelangelo Buonarroti (Codice Resta II). Cf. P. P. Rubens, *I disegni dell*—Ambrosiana, edition of the Banco Ambrosiano, Milan, 1975.

F. 250 inf. Various drawings.

F. 251 inf. Various drawings.

F. 252 inf. Architectural drawings, 16th and 17th centuries.

F. 253 inf. Figure drawings, 16th and 17th centuries.

F. 254 inf. Figure drawings, 16th and 17th centuries.

F. 255 inf. Figure drawings, 17th century.

F. 256-257-258 inf. Drawings by Giovanni Bettino Cignaroli, 18th century.

F. 261 inf. *Codice Resta* (cf. index of authors in *Studi Castiglioni*, 1957, pp. 311-328, prepared by M. Cogliati; *I disegni del Codice Resta*, edited by G. Bora, Silvana Editoriale, Milan, 1976.

In the collections F.— —————— G.— Fubini has in recent years brought together many drawings which earlier had no signature:

F. 262 inf. Drawings by Michelangelo Buonarroti and other great masters.

F. 263 inf. Drawings attributed to Leonardo and Leonardeschi.

F. 264 inf. Drawings by Albrecht Duerer. Cf. *Disegni e acquerelli di Albrecht Duerer e di Maestri Tedeschi*, Neri Pozza editore, 1968.

F. 265 inf. Drawings by great masters.

F. 266 inf. Drawings by great masters.

F. 267 inf. Drawings of London.

F. 268 inf. Various drawings.

F. 269 inf. Various drawings.

F. 270 inf. Various drawings.

F. 271 inf. Drawings by great masters.

F. 272 inf. Various drawings.

F. 273 inf. Various drawings.

F. 274 inf. Drawings attributed to Leonardo and Leonardeschi.

F. 275 inf. Drawings by Bisson.

F. 276-285 inf. Various drawings.

F. 290 inf. Various drawings.

P. 275 inf. Various drawings.

T. 189 sup. Paintings and drawings of cities, towns, castles and fortifications, 17th century.

T. 190 sup. Drawings of churches, water, streets, palaces, monsteries, etc. by the engineer Dionigi M. Ferrari and F. Bernardino Ferrari, 18th century.

T. 191 sup. Drawings of plants, sketches etc. of churches, monasteries, altars, houses, water, etc., some of them by the enbgineer Merlo.

T. l92-202 sup. Collection in eleven volumes by the engineer Bernardino Ferrari of manuscripts and prints pertaining to Navigli Grande, Bereguardo, Martesana, Paderno and Pavi, 17th century.

B. 58 inf. Project for the diversion of the Naviglio, compiled by the engineer Carlo Mira in 1865.

Z. 387-389 sup. Drawings of objects in the Settala Museum.

A provisional inventory of the drawings in the Ambrosiana is found in two manuscript volumes, *Continuazione Ceruti*, n. 86-87.

IV. Incunabula

The Ambrosiana has 2, 073 of them. They are listed in a manuscript catalogue (Cons. F. VII.8). Publication of a new catalogue has been begun under the direction of Dr. Felice Valsecchi; cf. *Fontes Ambrosiani*, Vol. XLVIII.

Other incunabula have come to the Ambrosiana as part of the L. V. Fossati Bellani Collection; these are minutely described in the catalogue of Pescarzoli (Cons. F. IV. 1-3).